THE BAPTIST IDENTITY
FOUR FRAGILE FREEDOMS

Smyth & Helwys Publishing, Inc.
6316 Peake Road
Macon, Georgia 31210-3960
1-800-747-3016

ISBN 978-1-880837-20-7

Library of Congress Cataloging-in-Publication Data
Shurden, Walter B.
The Baptist identity: four fragile freedoms / by Walter B. Shurden.
6x9" (15x23cm.) Includes
bibliographical references.
ISBN 978-1-880837-20-7

1. Baptists-Doctrines I. Title.
BX6331.2.S526 1993
286'.1-dc20 93-715
CIP

THE BAPTIST IDENTITY

Four Fragile Freedoms

WALTER B. SHURDEN

CONTENTS

for

Kay

"... they shook off this yoke of antichristian bondage,
and as the Lord's free people joined themselves
(by a covenant of the Lord) into a church estate,
in the fellowship of the gospel,
to walk in all His ways made known,
or to be made known unto them,
according to their best endeavours,
whatsoever it should cost them,
the Lord assisting them."

The Gainsborough Separatist Church, 1606,
led by John Smyth

INTRODUCTION

What makes a Baptist a Baptist? The ultimate and final answer, of course, is simple: membership in a local Baptist church. If the sisters and brothers vote you in, you are a Baptist. When a Baptist church accepts you, you are a Baptist. But there are all kinds of Baptist groups and Baptist churches! So what are the spiritual and theological marks of a Baptist? What are the generic "distinctives," the peculiar "convictions," the specific "ideals" that Baptists rally around and that make a Baptist a Baptist? What is the shape and the feel of Baptist Christianity?

Winthrop Hudson, one of Baptists' best historians and keenest twentieth-century interpreters, noted correctly that pioneer Baptists of seventeenth-century England did not set out to identify "Baptist distinctives." Their concern, coming out of the Puritan movement in England, was simply to be "faithful and obedient Christians" (Hudson, 6). Baptists wanted to know the mind and spirit of Christ as revealed in Holy Scripture. While Baptists, like all other Christian denominations, used biblical proof-texts to validate their positions, their primary approach was to derive general theological principles from their serious and sincere study of the Bible.

What I have tried to do in this book is to identify what H. Wheeler Robinson, noted British Baptist of the last generation, called "Baptist Principles," what American Baptists in a confessional statement called "convictional genes" (See Appendix VIII, 129), and what Edwin S. Gaustad, one of Baptists' most able contemporary historians, called "that distillation, that essence, that defining difference that constitutes being Baptist" (Gaustad, 85).

Martin E. Marty is a Lutheran church historian and America's source for almost all things religious. He wrote a fascinating article in the September 2, 1983, issue of *Christianity Today* with the arresting title, "Baptistification Takes Over." Marty created this awkward word, "baptistification," to describe what he called "the most dramatic shift in power style on the Christian scene in our time." He did not mean that people of other Christian denominations are running in droves to join Baptist churches. Nor did he mean that people are accepting immersion, the Baptist mode of baptism.

Marty meant, by the term "baptistification" and the phrase "dramatic shift," that a new religious *mood* was afoot in America. Catholics, Lutherans, Episcopalians, and others, said the noted church historian, were embracing this new mood. This mood, he said, stresses *freedom, choice,* and *voluntarism* in matters of faith. Correctly and significantly, Marty identified these very themes as hallmarks of the Baptist identity and focal points of the Baptist vision. These themes describe the spiritual instinct of historic Baptist life, the stackpole around which Baptist convictions develop.

"Baptistification" does not specify a particular Baptist doctrine; it does not speak to a unique Baptist distinctive. Rather it describes the Baptist *style* of faith. It is a particular *posture* of faith, a peculiar *attitude* toward the issues of faith. Baptistification is a *spirit* that pervades all of the Baptist principles or so-called Baptist distinctives. It is the spirit of FREEDOM.

The Baptist passion for freedom is a major reason why there is so much diversity in Baptist life. Baptists differ, and their differences are often broad and deep. But this has always been the case. In the very beginning of Baptist life in seventeenth-century England, for example, Baptists began in two separate and very distinct theological groups called General Baptists and Particular Baptists. Apart from other differences, General Baptists believed in free will and "falling from grace," and Particular Baptists believed in predestination and "once saved, always saved."

In the eighteenth-century American South, Regular Baptists and Separate Baptists were sharp contrasts in approach to worship, education, and even in life-style. In nineteenth-century England Charles Spurgeon and John Clifford represented major differences in their approaches to the Bible and historical understandings of Baptists.

And in the twentieth century, the same Baptist denomination that produced fundamentalists J. Frank Norris, T. T. Shields, and

W. B. Riley also begat liberals William Newton Clarke, Harry Emerson Fosdick, and later Carlyle Marney. Walter Rauschenbusch, the father of the social gospel, was a Baptist, but so is Billy Graham, probably the most effective evangelist in the history of Christendom. Martin Luther King, Jr., the soul of the American Civil Rights movement, was a Baptist; so was Governor Lester Maddox who chased blacks out of his restaurant.

In its May 14, 1984 issue, *U.S. News and World Report* reported on a survey of citizens around the country who were asked to rank the most influential persons in America outside of government. Three ordained Baptist ministers were listed in the top ten. Jerry Falwell, Jesse Jackson, and Billy Graham were ranked 7, 8, and 9 behind such familiar figures as Dan Rather and Lee Iacocca and ahead of such notables as Michael Jackson, David Rockefeller, and Henry Kissinger.

Jerry Falwell, Jesse Jackson, and Billy Graham! All are Baptists. Their ranking says two important things about Baptists today in America at the end of the twentieth century. The ranking says "prominence," but it also says "diversity."

President Bill Clinton, Vice-President Al Gore, and former President Jimmy Carter have intensified the prominence of Baptists in national and international life. Each of these three is considered moderate or centrist in his politics. But another prominent national politician who is also a Baptist is arch-conservative Senator Jesse Helms from North Carolina. Whatever else Baptists are, they are diverse!

The controversy that has shaken the Southern Baptist Convention for the last twelve years is one of the most recent examples of Baptist diversity. While diversity is threatening to some and downright devastating to others, it flows naturally from the Baptist preoccupation with the right of choice.

Despite their frustrating diversity, Baptists share some common convictions, however. One can certainly draw a Baptist profile or speak of a broad Baptist consensus. The problem comes when the profile is drawn too rigidly or the consensus is constructed around narrow principles that have not historically characterized the Baptist people generally.

The Baptist profile certainly can be sketched without using the categories I employ in this book. I seriously doubt, however, that the Baptist identity can be portrayed adequately without reference to the ideas inherent in the four Baptist freedoms and their attendant responsibilities that I outline here. It is important to me that the polarity of freedom and responsibility be underscored. The late Bishop Sheen is credited with saying that since the United States had a Statue of Liberty on the east coast the nation should also construct a Statue of Responsibility on the west coast. I second the motion! Fundamental to each of the Baptist freedoms I discuss is a solemn trust, a charge, an obligation, an undying responsibility.

John Hewett, the creative pastor of the First Baptist Church of Asheville, North Carolina, was the first person I heard use the term "Free and Faithful Baptists." It is a golden phrase. It captures the dialectic of liberty and loyalty, of change and continuity, of soul competency and the Lordship of Christ, of individualism and community so prominent in the Baptist heritage. While Hewett, to my knowledge, coined the phrase "Free and Faithful Baptists," the idea has been around for years in Baptist life. Penrose St. Amant, for example, used the same theme when he often summarized the Baptist identity with the phrase, "An open Bible and an open mind." Faithful and Free!

I first identified the four freedoms discussed in this book in the concluding chapter of my book *The Life of Baptists in the Life of the World,* published in 1985. In fact, at that time I identified five freedoms: Bible Freedom, Soul Freedom, Church Freedom, Religious Freedom (which I called Civil Freedom there), and Human Freedom. The emphasis on Human Freedom, in which I was trying to isolate the Baptist concern for both personal evangelism and social justice, is crucial to understanding Baptists. After further reflection, however, I have incorporated the idea of Human Freedom into my discussions of Soul Freedom and Church Freedom.

I arrived at these Baptist Freedoms by analyzing the sermons and addresses given by Baptists from around the world at the meetings of the Baptist World Alliance from 1905 to 1980. My conviction is that the Baptist World Alliance is the best place to look if one wants to mark major Baptist distinctives. The four freedoms that I use here to chisel the Baptist profile are: Bible Freedom, Soul Freedom, Church Freedom, and Religious Freedom.

BIBLE FREEDOM is the historic Baptist affirmation that the Bible, under the Lordship of Christ, must be central in the life of the individual and church and that Christians, with the best and most scholarly tools of inquiry, are both free and obligated to study and obey the Scripture.

SOUL FREEDOM is the historic affirmation of the inalienable right and responsibility of every person to deal with God without the imposition of creed, the interference of clergy, or the intervention of civil government.

CHURCH FREEDOM is the historic Baptist affirmation that local churches are free, under the Lordship of Christ, to determine their membership and leadership, to order their worship and work, to ordain whom they perceive as gifted for ministry, male or female, and to participate in the larger Body of Christ, of whose unity and mission Baptists are proudly a part.

RELIGIOUS FREEDOM is the historic Baptist affirmation of freedom *OF* religion, freedom *FOR* religion, and freedom *FROM* religion, insisting that Caesar is not Christ and Christ is not Caesar.

Each of these four freedoms relates to some major concept in the Christian faith. Bible Freedom, for example, focuses on the Lordship of Jesus Christ as revealed in the Scriptures and is the Baptist understanding of religious authority. Soul Freedom focuses on the primacy of the individual and reflects the Baptist approach to salvation, with implications for other areas as well. Church Freedom highlights the prominence of the believing community and the Baptist way of being and doing church. Religious Freedom is the Baptist approach to religious liberty and focuses on the relationship of religion to the state.

Near the time when I was completing this writing, I remembered a document issued by the Baptist Heritage Commission of the Baptist World Alliance in 1989 at Zagreb, Yugoslavia (now Croatia). Entitled "Towards A Baptist Identity," the statement was deliberately *descrip-*

tive rather than *creedal*. What amazed and pleased me were the five summary statements that concluded the document. Here is how it closes:

> Baptists are:
> —members of the whole Christian family who stress the experience of personal salvation through faith in Jesus, symbolized both in baptism and the Lord's Supper;
> —those who under the Lordship of Jesus Christ have bonded together in free local congregations, together seeking to obey Christ in faith and in life;
> —those who follow the authority of Scriptures in all matters of faith and practice;
> —those who have claimed religious liberty for themselves and all people;
> —those who believe that the Great Commission to take the Gospel to the whole world is the responsibility of the whole membership (as cited in Brackney, 149; see also Appendix I).

Only a glance will indicate that what I have designated as the "Four Baptist Freedoms" correspond almost exactly, though listed in a different order, with the Zagreb statement. My first affirmation of "Bible Freedom" is Zagreb's third; my "Soul Freedom" is its first; my "Church Freedom" is its second; and my "Religious Freedom" is its fourth. The fifth article in the Zagreb Statement on the Great Commission fits best in my judgment under a discussion of the church and its mission.

I have included the Zagreb Statement, along with seven other documents on the Baptist identity, in the appendixes of this book. Indeed, the appendixes constitute a very important part of this book, permitting the reader to check my interpretations of the Baptist profile against other major interpretations and descriptions.

Over the years many Baptist ministers, historians, and theologians have undertaken the task of describing and defining the Baptist identity. I have sought continuity with the historic Baptist character while casting the description of that character in categories relevant to the waning years of the twentieth century. I am particularly happy

that my interpretation matches so closely that of Baptist representatives from around the world as reflected in the Zagreb Statement.

I do not by any means want to suggest that Baptists are the only
Christians who adhere to these four freedoms. Happily, many others
do. What I do want to stress is that Baptists cannot be understood
without some reference to the ideas in these four freedoms, however
arranged, categorized, and described.

I have written this book with the hope that it can be used to
introduce new members of Baptist churches to the heritage of freedom
and faithfulness that they have entered. I hope, also, that it may be
used to remind and reawaken long-term Baptists to a heritage that
makes us proud far more times than it embarrasses us. I further hope
that it may be read by Christians in the larger Church of Christ who
would like to know the Baptist angle on our common faith in Jesus
of Nazareth.

No effort is made here to suggest that Baptists are the only ones
or even the best ones God has. I have never believed we were the only
ones. I may have at one time believed we were the best, but I have
repented of that a thousand times and with good reason. Tribalism,
like all other provincialisms, has to die. I do not decry the death of
tribalism; but neither do I deny the pull of home. For me, the larger
Baptist family has been my home and my little corner of the forty-
acre field of Christendom. While I do not applaud everything about
my faith family, I hope I am not flirting again with tribalism when
I say that at the center of my being there is something about being
Baptist, properly understood, that is both freeing and fulfilling.

BIBLIOGRAPHY

Brackney, William H., editor, *Faith, Life, and Witness: The Papers of the Study and
Research Division of the Baptist World Alliance, 1986–1990*. Birmingham,
Alabama: Samford University Press, 1990.

Hudson, Winthrop Still, *Baptist Convictions*. Valley Forge: The Judson Press, 1963.

Gaustad, Edwin S., "Toward A Baptist Identity in the Twenty-First Century," in
     William H. Brackney, editor, *Discovering Our Baptist Heritage*. Valley Forge:
     The American Baptist Historical Society, 1985.

CHAPTER ONE

BIBLE FREEDOM

BIBLE FREEDOM is the historic Baptist affirmation that the Bible, under the Lordship of Christ, must be central in the life of the individual and church and that Christians, with the best and most scholarly tools of inquiry, are both free and obligated to study and obey the Scripture.

INTRODUCTION

Baptists have no monopoly on the Bible. There is no "Baptist Bible." Baptists claim the same sixty-six books of the Bible as the written word of God as do most other Christians. Those books were accepted as canonical and authoritative by Christians by the fourth century. Since Baptists did not appear until the seventeenth century, we are beneficiaries of the Bible from the larger Christian movement.

Baptists are not only beneficiaries of the Bible from the Church Universal; they have inherited many of their most important beliefs from the larger Church. For example, there is no distinctive "Baptist" concept of God, Christ, the Holy Spirit, or the Bible. These classic doctrines were formed long before Baptists came on the scene. Even those principles that are often dubbed "Baptist distinctives" are gifts to us from the Protestant Reformers. Baptists believe fervently in the authority of scripture, but for that we can say thanks to Martin Luther. Nor did we invent salvation by grace alone or the priesthood of believers. We were not even the first ones to get to the idea of a believers' church or religious liberty.

One can, of course, contend that all these Baptist emphases are found in the Bible. They are. But we got them from the Bible by way of some other Christians. One of the first, and often unacknowledged, features of the Baptist tradition is its ecumenical relationship to the broader Christian tradition. Baptists, like most other Christians, are a dependent people. Recognition of our dependence is no small matter simply because some Baptists have sought erroneously to divorce our biblical interpretations, our theological commitments, and our historical origins too completely from the ecumenical church.

This attempted divorce has had tragic consequences for Baptists. It is time for Baptists who acknowledge the authority of scripture for faith and practice to confess our oneness with and our dependency on the larger Body of Christ. This confession of oneness and dependency calls us to a fresh commitment to Bible Freedom.

BIBLE FREEDOM MEANS FREEDOM "UNDER"

The problem of Jesus, recorded in John's Gospel (5:37-40), still exists today. Some people search the scriptures because they think that in them they will find eternal life. These people fail to understand that the scriptures testify of Jesus. The preeminence of Jesus over scripture is clearly noted in Hebrews 1:1-2. Scripture points beyond itself to Immanuel, the Christ, God with us.

Christians stand, therefore, with an open Bible "under" the Lordship of Jesus Christ. When they began in the early 1600s in England, Baptists insisted on Jesus as the only Lord of their lives. For them Jesus was the center of the biblical revelation. Everything in the Hebrew Scriptures reached its climax in the Nazarene Carpenter. Everything in the church subsequent to his life, death, and resurrection looked back to him as the focal point of faith.

This Baptist emphasis on the ultimate authority of Jesus Christ as mediated through the Bible is clearly reflected in Baptist confessional statements. The "Declaration of Principle" of The Baptist Union of Great Britain and Ireland says that the Union is based, among others, on the conviction "that our Lord and Saviour Jesus Christ, God manifest in the flesh, is the sole and absolute authority in all matters pertaining to faith and practice, as revealed in the Holy Scriptures...."

Likewise, two of the most important Baptist confessions issued in twentieth-century America mirror the same opinion. One of these, issued in celebration of the one hundred and fiftieth anniversary of the first national Baptist organization founded in America (The Triennial Convention), is entitled "Baptist Distinctives and Diversities." A committee composed of a representative of Southern Baptists, American Baptists, Canadian Baptists, black Baptists, Seventh Day Baptists, and the North American Baptist General Conference wrote this significant doctrinal document in 1964. The first article in this statement discusses the issue of "Authority." The opening sentences of this article read as follows: "The foundation truth upon which Baptists build is the Lordship of Christ over the individual believer. All other authorities are judged by the authority of the Son of God."

Also in 1964, and in celebration of the same occasion, Ralph A. Herring, pastor of the First Baptist Church in Winston-Salem, North Carolina, chaired a committee composed of eighteen Southern Baptist Convention leaders and scholars. This committee issued a marvelous statement of Baptist distinctives entitled "Baptist Ideals." Like "Baptist Distinctives and Diversities," "Baptist Ideals" opens by saying, "The ultimate source of Christian authority is Jesus Christ the Lord."

Jesus, for Baptists, constitutes the norm by which the Bible is to be interpreted. "The Baptist Faith and Message" puts it bluntly and unequivocally: "The criterion by which the Bible is to be interpreted is Jesus Christ." Why is Jesus, for Baptists, the only norm for biblical interpretation? Because "Jesus is Lord" was the earliest and primary New Testament confession (Rom 10:9; Phil 2:11). For Baptists, therefore, Jesus is the ultimate source of Christian authority and the foundation truth upon which they attempt to build their lives and their churches.

Baptists insisted on freedom of access to the Bible and freedom of interpretation of the Bible precisely because it is the only means of arriving at the mind of the Lord Christ. Again, in the language of "The Baptist Faith and Message," "the sole authority for faith and practice among Baptists is Jesus Christ whose will is revealed in the Holy Scriptures." Jesus, for Baptists, as for most other Christians, is far more than a mere historical person of the first century. He is the

Living Lord who still directs and guides his people. And so the Bible, interpreted under the guidance of the Holy Spirit, continues to make the will of Christ known.

BIBLE FREEDOM MEANS FREEDOM "FOR"

Because of the power of scripture to make the will of God known to us, the Bible is a dynamic book. As people read and interpret scripture under the guidance of the Holy Spirit, their lives are transformed. God's word is not limited to scripture (Rom 1:20; 2:15; Ps 19:1-4). Yet, the word of God that is "living and active" (Heb 4:12a) is certainly heard through scripture, and, as a result, "thoughts and intentions of the heart" are judged (Heb 4:12b). In order for Christians to live obediently under the Lordship of Christ, they must be free to respond to the living word of God.

Baptists wanted freedom of access to the Bible "for" the purpose of continuing obedience to the Word of God. Baptists began with a dynamic, rather than static, understanding of the Bible. Unrestrained freedom to follow the Bible wherever it might lead was of first importance to Baptists.

John Smyth is considered to be the father of the modern Baptist denomination. A man with the most common of names, he had uncommon courage. Educated as an Anglican clergyman at Cambridge University in England, he became increasingly dissatisfied with that church and joined a group of Separatists (people who had separated from the Church of England) at the town of Gainsborough.

In 1606 Smyth drew up a brief covenant for this group. William Bradford, one of their number and later a Pilgrim Father, described their break with their Anglican past and their remarkable openness to God's message in the future:

> they shook off this yoke of antichristian bondage, and as the Lord's free people joined themselves (by a covenant of the Lord) into a church estate, in the fellowship of the gospel, to walk in all His ways made known, or to be made known unto them, according to

their best endeavours, whatsoever it should cost them, the Lord
assisting them. (Bradford, 9)

As "the Lord's free people," they pledged themselves "to walk
in all his ways made known, or *to be made known unto them* ...
whatsoever it should cost them." These "free people" wanted freedom
to obey new truth and light that might break forth from God's Word.
This commitment to the ongoing quest for truth eventually led
Smyth, for example, to the cardinal Baptist conviction of believer's
baptism.

For Baptists, the Bible is and always has been the final authority.
It is the final authority in moral responsibility, in theological beliefs,
and in human relationships. The Bible is final, but human understanding of the Bible is never final or complete or finished. That was
the Gainsborough principle! And as the great English Baptist historian, Ernest A. Payne, said, it "is of fundamental importance for an
understanding of Baptist life at its best" (Payne, 19).

Baptists did not begin and apparently did not intend to live out
their faith as a static, rigidly fixed and inflexible group of disciples.
They did not arrive at *The* truth in every area of life and then determine to pass it on to succeeding generations. What they arrived at
was an attitude of openness to the ongoing study of the Bible under
the guidance of the Living Lord of the Church. When Southern
Baptists revised the "Statement of the Baptist Faith and Message" in
1963, they clearly intended this attitude to continue. A portion of
the revised 1963 confession says:

> Baptists are a people who profess a living faith. This faith is rooted
> and grounded in Jesus Christ who is "the same yesterday, and to-
> day, and for ever." Therefore, the sole authority for faith and prac-
> tice among Baptists is Jesus Christ whose will is revealed in the Holy
> Scriptures.
>
> A living faith must experience a growing understanding of
> truth and must be continually interpreted and related to the needs
> of each new generation.

"A living faith!" "A growing understanding of truth!" The Gainsborough principle was alive and well in Kansas City as recently as
1963! It is this frame of mind and this posture of faith that not only
allows but encourages diversity.

Some may ask, "Is this approach not fraught with danger?" And
the answer is a candid "Of Course!" The alternative, however, is
fraught with more than danger; it is fraught with death resulting from
an unbending dogmatism. Built into the Gainsborough approach is
the idea that our understandings and interpretations of the Bible
change; the Bible, however, remains the Word of the Living God.
With this birthright of freedom and faithfulness to the Bible as the
Word of God, no Christian communion should be better able to meet
the changing challenges of the contemporary world than Baptists.

BIBLE FREEDOM MEANS FREEDOM "FROM"

Early Baptists echoed Martin Luther's conviction-filled affirmation of
sola scriptura, "scripture alone." And they did so because they wanted
to be free "from" all other religious authorities. Baptists began by saying, "This Lord and no more!" No pope, no king, and no bishop
could usurp the Lordship of Christ. Baptists also began by saying,
"This Book and no more!" By which they meant that all creeds, confessions, and doctrinal statements of ecclesiastical bodies and religious
councils could not usurp the authority of the Bible.

Over the years some Baptists have almost forgotten it. So it must
be said again and it must be said loudly this time: BAPTISTS ARE A
NON-CREEDAL PEOPLE! There is no *The* Baptist Creed or *The*
Baptist Confession of Faith or *The* Baptist Church Covenant.
Historically, Baptists have resisted any and all creeds. And they have
for two very good reasons. First, no one doctrinal statement can
summarize adequately the biblical mandate for behavior and belief.
It is better, therefore, to stay with the Bible alone. Second, Baptists
have feared creeds because of the seemingly inevitable tendency to
make the creed the *norm* and then to *force* compliance to the creed.
This is precisely what happened in the recent controversy over the

Bible in the Southern Baptist Convention. When creeds replace the Bible, we lose both the Bible and the freedom of approach to the Bible.

To say that Baptists are anti-creedal is certainly not to suggest that Baptists reject the teachings of the classic creedal statements that have evolved from the broader Christian community. Indeed, when the revered eighty-year old Alexander Maclaren took the chair to preside over the first international gathering of the Baptist World Alliance in 1905 in London, England, he called upon his audience to identify with historic Christianity. Here is what Maclaren said and what he called upon Baptists at that world meeting to do:

> I should like that there should be no misunderstanding on the part of the English public, or the American public . . . as to where we stand in the continuity of the historic Church. And I should like the first act of this Congress to be the audible and unanimous acknowledgment of our Faith. So I have suggested that, given your consent, it would be an impressive and a right thing, and would clear away a good many misunderstandings and stop the mouth of a good deal of slander—if we here and now, in the face of the world, not as a piece of coercion or discipline, but as a simple acknowledgment of where we stand and what we believe, would rise to our feet and, following the lead of your President, would repeat the Apostles' Creed. (as cited in Shurden, 17)

Baptists from several continents stood and repeated slowly and deliberately the whole of the Apostles' Creed. In no way, however, could their action be mistaken for creedalism.

To say, therefore, that Baptists are historically an anti-creedal people is not to divorce the Baptist faith from the faith of the ecumenical church. Nor is it to overlook the obvious fact that Baptists have periodically adopted doctrinal statements of their own. W. J. McGlothlin's *Baptist Confessions of Faith*, William L. Lumpkin's book by the same title, and G. Keith Parker's *Baptists in Europe: History and Confessions of Faith* are important collections of numerous Baptist confessional documents. The very fact, however, that Baptists have adopted *many* different confessions is a sign of freedom from creedal conformity and of the ongoing quest for truth represented by the Gainsborough principle. W. J. McGlothlin made this point in his 1911 book:

> Being congregational and democratic in church government, Baptists have naturally been very free in making, changing, and using Confessions. There has never been among them any ecclesiastical authority which could impose a Confession upon their churches or other bodies. Their Confessions are, strictly speaking, statements of what a certain group of Baptists, large or small, did believe at a given time, rather than a creed which any Baptist must believe at all times in order to hold ecclesiastical position or to be considered a Baptist. In the latter sense there has been no Baptist creed. (McGlothlin, xii)

In speaking of Baptists and their confessional statements, one should also note that some parts of the Baptist family have been reluctant to adopt any type of extensive doctrinal statement. The American Baptist Churches, U.S.A., for example, adopted only the briefest of statements in 1922 during the fundamentalist modernist controversy, and it remains the official position of that part of the Baptist family. In order to avoid a binding doctrinal manifesto, Cornelius Woelfkin introduced a resolution that year that stated "that the New Testament is the all-sufficient ground of our faith and practice, and we need no other statement" (as cited in Torbet, 430). The resolution passed two to one.

A careful reading of McGlothlin, Lumpkin, and Parker will demonstrate that when Baptists have adopted theological documents they have carefully named them so as not to ascribe too much authority to them. Baptists usually have steered clear of the word "creed" for that very reason. The term most often used by Baptists to declare their faith has been "confession," but other descriptions have been used as well. For example, The Baptist Union of Great Britain and Ireland has a very brief "Declaration of Principle." What is popularly known among Southern Baptists as "The Baptist Faith and Message" is more correctly entitled "A Statement of the Baptist Faith and Message." It is "A Statement." It is not "The Creed." The difference is significant for Baptists.

Not only have Baptists carefully named their statements; they have also painstakingly circumscribed the authority of the confessions. This was clearly the case with "A Statement of The Baptist Faith and Message" adopted in 1963. The preface affirmed that the articles of the statement were not to be regarded "as complete statements of our faith, having any quality of finality or infallibility." Moreover, it said that "confessions are only guides in interpretation, having no authority over the conscience, . . . and are not to be used to hamper freedom of thought or investigation in other realms of life."

The fact that this statement has been sorely abused in recent years so as to enforce a narrow theology only confirms the historic Baptist suspicion of creedal statements. The pattern of a growing restrictionism, documentable in Christian history generally and made explicit in Southern Baptist history, goes like this. First, strong affirmations opposing all creeds are made, such as the one by Baptists at the founding of the Southern Baptist Convention in 1845: "We have constructed for our basis no new creed; acting in this matter upon a Baptist aversion for all creeds but the Bible" (*Annual*, 19). Second, a group, such as fundamentalists, emerges and calls for a strict theological orthodoxy. Third, they issue a call for a confessional statement, as Southern Baptist fundamentalists did in 1925, to guard the orthodoxy. Fourth, they call for the imposition of the statement to guarantee the orthodoxy. By that time Baptists have left their heritage. Baptists, if they are to be historic Baptists, are required to resurrect their tradition of anti creedalism and to resist statements about the Bible that limit access to the Bible and that codify human understanding of biblical theology.

BIBLE FREEDOM MEANS FREEDOM "OF"

God has spoken to humanity "in many and various ways" (Heb 1:1). In Jesus Christ, God spoke with clarity. Yet, God has never dictated that each individual should agree precisely on what God has said. Even in the Gospels, four distinct views of Jesus are expressed. After

Luke acknowledged that others had undertaken to complete a narrative of the Jesus events, he wrote, "I too decided . . . to write an orderly account" (Luke 1:3). Each writer agrees that Jesus was the long awaited Anointed One of God, although each interprets his life and ministry from a unique perspective, even relating details differently. The Gospels are portraits, not photographs of Jesus.

Matthew, for example, sees Jesus as the new Moses, one who brings a new interpretation of God's law from a new and different "mountain." Mark portrays Jesus as the Son of God who confronts and exorcises evil. For Luke, Jesus is Savior for those on the floor of life, the outcasts, the ostracized, and those snubbed by the religious. John portrays Jesus as the Divine Word who comes from above to bring God's grace to sinners. While the Gospels differ in their interpretations of Jesus because of their specific purposes and particular audiences, none was wrong. And contrary to Marcion, no one of them, including Luke, was THE right one.

Baptists have no formal or informal teaching office that hands down correct biblical interpretation. Freedom "of" interpretation by each individual believer is fundamental to Baptist thought. The Bible is open to all believers. If believers are to be guided by Holy Scripture, believers must be free to interpret the Bible.

This idea of the right of private interpretation of scripture is no Johnny-come-lately in twentieth-century Baptist life. In 1846, W. B. Johnson, the founder and first president of the Southern Baptist Convention, published a fascinating little book that among other things, opposed confessions of faith as a basis of Baptist union, advocated women deacons, described the church as a "holy priesthood," and lobbied for the principle of "equal rights" in the church. In the "Introduction" to his book, Johnson identified what we have come to refer to as "Baptist Distinctives," what he called "the true fundamental principles of the gospel of Christ."

Johnson listed five specific convictions that characterized Baptists in the South in the middle of the nineteenth century. These five "fundamentals" were (1) the sovereignty of God in salvation, (2) "the supreme authority of the scripture," (3) "the right of each individual to judge for himself in his views of truth as taught in the scriptures,"

(4) democratic church government, and (5) believers' baptism (Johnson, 16).

By stressing "the right of each individual" to judge for oneself the meaning of the Bible, this first president of the Southern Baptist Convention was not alone. Baptists before and after him, when upholding historic Baptist fundamentals, have lobbied for this principle. Torn by theological controversy in the latter part of the nineteenth century, the Baptist Union of Great Britain and Ireland affirmed their faith in "the Divine Inspiration and Authority of the Holy Scriptures as the supreme and sufficient rule of our faith and practice: *and the right and duty of individual judgment in the interpretation of it*" (as cited in Parker, 280).

As one would expect, the absence of any single, final or official interpretation of scripture has created diversity, consternation, and even conflict between Baptists themselves. For example, the Zagreb Statement of 1990, in speaking of the Baptist campaign for "liberation of opinion," said, "Such freedom has led the Baptists to be a diverse people with no over-arching rule demanding common thought or practice among them" (as cited in Brackney, 148). Likewise, the committee members, representing six different Baptist groups in North America, who wrote "Baptist Distinctives and Diversities," observed that in light of "the historic Baptist emphasis upon soul-liberty and freedom of conscience," one should not be surprised to discover considerable theological and practical diversity among Baptists.

They then identified a number of "disagreements and differences of emphasis among Baptists." One of these "disagreements and differences" concerned the Bible itself. Declaring that "all Baptists acknowledge the inspiration and authority of Scripture," the authors of this important document went on to say,

> It is clear that there is great diversity among us in regard to principles of interpretation, the nature and manner of inspiration, the precise way in which Scripture is understood in the light of the final authority of Christ Himself. Problems of authorship and historicity, the nature of Biblical language and the meaning of terms such as "literal" and "symbolic," the legitimacy of a scholarly approach to

the Scriptures and the limits of such a treatment of the Bible—all these are matters on which no complete unanimity is to be found among Baptists. This is not necessarily to be deplored provided such differences are anchored in a sincere loyalty to the Scriptures and to Jesus Christ as Lord and Saviour. Nor can Baptists with their emphasis upon freedom rightly expect complete uniformity in the language used to express our deepest convictions about God and Christ. (Appendix II, 91)

So the believer's right of private interpretation of the Bible often brings conflict with it. Jesus acknowledged as much when he prefaced his interpretations of Hebrew Scripture in his famous Sermon on the Mount with the statement, "Do not think that I have come to abolish the law and the prophets" (Matt 5:17). Legalistic creedalism often interprets *differences* of interpretation as *destruction* of the Bible itself. Such differences also bring, however, the weighty responsibility to study and seek to understand the Bible. This demands the best biblical scholarship as an aid to interpretation. The right of private interpretation does not mean that any or every interpretation is correct. It does not mean that the Bible means anything or everything or nothing.

The privilege of personal interpretation of the Bible is hard work! Some questions must be asked and answered. What did this biblical statement mean in its original setting? When was it written? Under what circumstances? What thought patterns dominated the world of the writer? To understand the Bible, one should know something about the history *of* the Bible, the history *within* the Bible, and good principles for interpreting the Bible today. Some Baptists want the privilege of personal interpretation of the Bible, but they do not want to go to the trouble to be good interpreters. Too many Baptists let others do their Bible study for them. We must distinguish between the noble privilege of interpreting the Bible for ourselves and the responsibility of working hard at determining what its authors intended it to mean.

BIBLIOGRAPHY

Annual, Southern Baptist Convention, 1845.

Brackney, William H., editor, *Faith, Life, and Witness: The Papers of the Study and Research Division of the Baptist World Alliance, 1986–1990.* Birmingham, Alabama: Samford University Press, 1990.

Bradford, William, *Of Plymouth Plantation: 1620–1647.* Edited with an introduction and notes by Samuel Eliot Morison. New York: Alfred A. Knopf, 1982.

Johnson, William Bullein, *The Gospel Developed Through the Government and Order of the Churches of Jesus Christ.* Richmond: H. K. Ellyson, 1846.

Lumpkin, William L., *Baptist Confessions of Faith.* Revised edition. Valley Forge: The Judson Press, 1969.

McGlothlin, W. J. *Baptist Confessions of Faith.* Valley Forge: Judson Press, 1911.

Parker, G. Keith, *Baptists in Europe: History and Confessions of Faith.* Nashville: Broadman Press, 1982.

Payne, Ernest A., *The Fellowship of Believers: Baptist Thought and Practice Yesterday and Today.* London: The Carey Kingsgate Press, 1952.

Shurden, Walter B., editor, *The Life of Baptists in the Life of the World.* Nashville: Broadman Press, 1985.

Tarbet, Robert G., *A History of the Baptists.* Third edition. Valley Forge: Judson Press, 1950.

CHAPTER TWO

SOUL FREEDOM

SOUL FREEDOM is the historic Baptist affirmation of the inalienable right and responsibility of every person to deal with God without the imposition of creed, the interference of clergy, or the intervention of civil government.

INTRODUCTION

What I am here calling Soul Freedom has been described in Baptist life by a variety of terms and phrases. "Individual competency," "the competency of the soul before God," "personal faith," "soul liberty," "spiritual religion," "believer priesthood," "conversion by conviction," "experiential religion," "individualism in religion," and even "sanctified individualism" are efforts at capturing the substance of the idea of Soul Freedom. Breathing through all these terms, however, are essential ideas for an understanding of Baptist spirituality.

THE CENTRALITY OF THE INDIVIDUAL

When Jesus confronted his disciples about his identity—"who do people say that the Son of Man is? (Matt 16:13)"—he was accenting the importance of personal response to his ministry and negating the notion that an authentic interpretation of him can come by survey or majority vote. Jesus recognized that people perceived him differently and responded to him in different ways.

Soul Freedom affirms the sacredness of individual choice. Baptists have often been accused of being excessively "individualistic." As we shall see when we come to the Baptist emphasis on the church, individualism is far from the total picture for Baptists. For the most part, however, Baptists never crouch in a defensive position when the charge of individualism is hurled at them. With all of its inherent weakness, individualism is to a great degree a Baptist badge of honor.

A strong streak of stubborn individualism weaves its way through the Baptist story, and anyone who deletes it both distorts our history and abuses our understanding of the Christian faith. Some, mistakenly thinking that an emphasis on individualism would destroy community in Baptist life, have panned E. Y. Mullins' emphasis on soul competence, thinking it too individualistic. But contemporary Baptist historian William Brackney is closer to the truth when he says of Mullins and his emphasis that "he identified an important aspect of Baptist identity" (Brackney, 71). That old story told as a joke and quoted by Carlyle Marney, a Baptist individualist if ever there was one, has truth in it: "The rabbi begins, 'Thus saith the *Lord!*' The priest begins, 'As the *Church* has always said . . . .' The average Protestant begins, 'Now, brothers and sisters, it seems to *Me*. . . .'" Baptists are among the most individualistic of Protestants.

The Baptist emphasis on the individual is based on the biblical affirmation that every human being is created in the image of God. Biblical interpreters and theologians have debated for years the precise meaning of Genesis 1:26—"Let us make humankind in our image." Baptists have agreed, however, that whatever else it means, it speaks, as does Psalm 8, clearly of the infinite worth and dignity of each individual.

Baptists assert that each individual is created in the image of God. Each individual, therefore, is competent under God to make moral, spiritual, and religious decisions. Not only is the individual privileged to make those decisions, the individual alone is *responsible* for making those decisions. "Who do *you* ... ?"

I referred previously to "Baptist Ideals," the excellent confessional document issued in 1964. The second article of "Baptist Ideals," entitled simply "The Individual," speaks eloquently and passionately of the individual's worth, competence, and freedom. Significantly, the last article in the document speaks of "Our Continuing Task" to preserve the distinctive witness of Baptist principles. Guess what the authors placed as a first priority in preserving the Baptist witness? They called it the "Centrality of the Individual."

THE PRIMACY OF THE PERSONAL

Jesus understood that the public had vastly diverse perceptions of him, but he was most interested in what the disciples thought. His question, "But who do you say that I am?" (Matt 16:15) called for personal response. He was not looking for group response. Jesus did not ask his disciples, "What do the prophets say about me?" He did not quiz them as to the official position of the Hebrew scriptures regarding his identity. He invited personal response based on voluntary commitment.

In the Baptist faith tradition, individualism in religious matters manifests itself at the very beginning of the Christian life. Baptists insist that saving faith is personal, not impersonal. It is relational, not ritualistic. It is direct, not indirect. It is a lonely, frightened, sinful individual before an almighty, loving, and gracious God.

History helps us understand the Baptist position. A century before Baptists emerged in England, Martin Luther challenged the medieval theology of Roman Catholicism. That theology taught that God's grace was centered *in* the church and mediated *through* the sacraments *by* the priests. Grace was institutionally based, sacramentally received, and indirectly mediated. Luther said, "No!"

A century later Baptists joined the chorus, claiming that the individual comes before God personally, directly, and voluntarily. They were affirming the centrality of the individual over the institutional, the priority of the personal over the sacramental, and the preeminence of direct access over indirect access to God.

Six hundred years before Jesus gave the individual invitation to "follow me," the prophet Jeremiah preached the primacy of the personal in matters of faith. In what has been called "the gospel before the gospel" Jeremiah promised a new covenant. "I will put my law within them, and I will write it on their hearts," (Jer 31:33). With pen in hand God would write not on stone but on the inner being of the individual, prophesied Jeremiah. Why? Because knowledge of God is direct, dynamic, and personal. Fellowship with God comes by way of individual relationship and not through creed and ceremony. Jeremiah's prophecy of the Divine-human relationship was so important for early Christians that the writer of Hebrews quoted it not once but twice in a space of two chapters (see Heb 8:8-12; 10:16-17).

Soul Freedom or "individual competency" has never meant human self-sufficiency. Baptists have never come close to saying that individuals are capable or competent to save themselves. Basic to the Baptist understanding of the gospel is the grace of God (Eph 2:8-9; Titus 3:5-6). But that grace is always personally appropriated. No proxy can fetch grace for you. We are saved one by one, person by person, and individual by individual.

This is no effort to minimize community. It is an effort to make faith meaningful. The theme of the *individual in community* is a cardinal biblical theme, present in both Old and New Testaments. But salvation is not church by church, community by community, or nation by nation. It is lonely soul by lonely soul. E.Y. Mullins, one of the best Baptist theologians of this century, was right to speak of "the principle of individualism in religion" (Mullins, 93).

Walter Rauschenbusch, the father of the social gospel, in maybe the greatest of all "Why I Am A Baptist" sermons, made the same point as Mullins, but he called it "experimental religion" (as cited in Stealey, 166.) Rauschenbusch pointed out that personal experience lies behind the Baptist understanding of conversion, the Baptist prerequisite for entering the ministry, the Baptist requirement for church membership, baptism, and the Lord's Supper.

CONVERSION BY CONVICTION

Simon Peter's spontaneous response to Jesus' personal question was confessional: "You are the Messiah, the Son of the living God" (Matt 16:16). Jesus did not exert external pressure on Peter to respond in this manner. Nobody scripted his confession. Jesus celebrated Peter's response as being motivated by spiritual conviction: "Blessed are you, Simon son of Jonah! For flesh and blood has not revealed this to you, but my Father in heaven" (Matt 16:17).

Peter's confession was a free choice response to Divine initiative and was stated in his own words. Peter's confession, born of conviction, is part of what Baptists mean by soul freedom. Soul Freedom even allows for mistaken choices and wrong interpretations. Simon was right in proclaiming Jesus as Messiah, but he was wrong in resisting Jesus' Messiahship as one of suffering. Jesus said to him, "Get behind me, Satan! (Matt 16:23)" Jesus permitted Peter to be both advocate and adversary.

Soul Freedom means the right to choose. Faith is voluntary. No one is forced to believe because no one can be forced to believe. Some words cannot be put together. "Forced love!" There is no such thing. You can force labor. You can force slavery. But you cannot "force" someone to love God. The voluntary nature of faith is crucial to the Baptist identity. To try to make someone believe what they honestly cannot believe exploits both the individual and the biblical meaning of faith.

John Cuddy works across the street from the First Baptist Church in Macon, Georgia. He is the Roman Catholic priest at St. Joseph's Catholic Church and one of the most respected ministers in the town. We had him over to First Baptist one Wednesday night to tell us all about the Catholics. During a question and answer session someone asked him, "Father Cuddy, what one thing do you admire the most about Baptists?" Quickly and without struggling for a response, he answered, "Freedom." Bull's eye! While he did not elaborate, he could have meant several things—the freedom of private interpretation of the Bible, the freedom of democratic church government, the freedom from creeds, or freedom from the state. But he also could have meant the freedom to choose to believe. It is at the heart of the Baptist genius. Conversion, for Baptists, is always a matter of the soul's conviction.

Soul Freedom, like all other Baptist freedoms, has a goal in view. Freedom is such an important ingredient in the human enterprise that one could philosophically justify freedom for freedom's sake. Baptists had more in mind, however, than simply breaking free from chains that held them back. Freedom had purpose for Baptists. They wanted freedom from a state-enforced religion because they thought that the freedom of the human spirit was worth saving. They rebelled against the priority of institutionalism because they believed that the priority of the individual was worth saving.

Running through the Dallas-Ft.Worth airport to catch a commuter flight, I could not help but see a slogan printed on a sweatshirt. "MAKE UP YOUR OWN MIND!" it screamed. "Choose this day whom you will serve (Josh 24:15)" is the ancient Hebrew version of that slogan. Both exhortations imply the freedom of choice. More specifically, however, they highlight the responsibility for personal decision. Because we are all accountable to God (Rom 14:12), we are also responsible for spiritual and religious matters.

Some people, it seems, will do almost anything to avoid the responsibility for their lives. They will quote other people, talk like other people, let other people talk for them, or even choose for them. Sooner or later, however, that question from Jesus is mine and yours to answer: "But who do *you* say that I am?" The Baptist word for the world is that each individual is free to answer and is responsible for answering. The old spiritual places the emphasis where Baptists have wanted it: "It's not my mother; it's not my brother, but it's me, O Lord, standing in the need of prayer."

Periodically throughout their history, some Baptists, especially fundamentalists, unintentionally advocate an impersonal faith by placing rigid emphasis on correct belief. While they would agree in principle with the idea that "Baptists are non-creedal," they often create a theological "law of the Medes and Persians," an unwritten but often heavy-handed creedalism. Correct and accurate intellectual comprehension of the Christian faith has never been the basic demand in historic Baptist life, however. Five right responses to five right questions never made a Christian out of anyone. This is rationalistic, not experiential faith. "Even the demons," said James (Jas 2:19), have this kind of faith.

Because "Soul Freedom" argues that faith must be personal, it does not prescribe *one* specific kind of conversion. Individuals come to obedience to Jesus in different ways. If faith is personal and individualistic, it will always manifest itself in different shapes and forms and styles. Many Baptists in America, influenced heavily by revivalistic religion, think of conversion as of one type—spontaneous, immediate, and somewhat emotional. This one-sided preoccupation with instant conversion often neglects the subsequent growth and maturation of Christians. More tragically, however, it ignores the fact that Christian conversions are not all of one type.

I am one of those people who can take you to the place and drive a nail where I first met the Holy in life. I remember being surprised, therefore, when I heard the late Dr. W. O. Vaught, longtime pastor of the Immanuel Baptist Church in Little Rock, Arkansas, and spiritual mentor to President Bill Clinton, say in a sermon, "I do not remember the day or the hour or the place when I first met Christ." I also heard a Baptist seminary professor say, "My earliest memory is that of sitting on a piano bench beside my Mother and singing 'Jesus Loves Me.'" "I never remember a time," said the theologian, "when I did not believe that he loved me or that I loved him."

Paul's Damascus Road experience is a story of profound transformation, but for too long some Baptists have held it up as the only viable model of conversion. To take Soul Freedom seriously, we must be prepared to accept the diversity of religious experience. In fact, the best safeguard against uniformity of religious experience is what H. Wheeler Robinson described as "the clear declaration of the individuality of faith" (Robinson, 20).

BAPTISM FOR BELIEVERS

Christ's Church is built upon the foundation of individual souls freely responding to the incarnate Son of the Living God (Matt 16:18). Through personal confessions of faith, lives are changed and the "gates of hell" are razed.

In Baptist life, these followers of Christ make a public statement of their faith through the waters of baptism. Ask the average person what is the distinguishing characteristic of the Baptist denomination, and they will probably answer with something about the *way* Baptists baptize. While true today that Baptists universally practice baptism by immersion, their earliest concern regarding baptism was not the *mode* of baptism or *how* one should be baptized. Their earliest concern was with the *subject* of baptism or *who* was being baptized. Baptists' ultimate goal was a church composed of believers only, but they could not get to that goal apart from the personal faith of individuals who made up that church.

The earliest Baptists began baptizing believers before they began baptizing believers by immersion. The Baptist denomination began with two Englishmen by the name of John Smyth and Thomas Helwys in the early 1600s. Smyth, a clergyman, and Helwys, a layman, led a small group of former Anglicans in search of religious freedom from Gainsborough, England, to Amsterdam, Holland, in 1607/8. By 1609 Smyth became convinced that baptism should be administered to believers only. Since he and his followers had been baptized as infants when they could not choose Christ, Smyth first baptized himself by "pouring" water on his head, and he then baptized the others. So you can see that their primary concern was not the mode but the subject of baptism.

Their first concern was believers' baptism. But the point to underscore is that even this fundamental Baptist idea is derivative. It comes from another, more basic and essential, idea—that of a personal and voluntary faith. Baptists wanted the person being baptized to be able to make a free and voluntary choice for Christ. Baptism was a sign, therefore, that one had made a pledge to a new purpose. It was a dramatic statement that "Christ is Lord."

In fact, in the New Testament baptism appears to be what many Baptists refer to today as "a public profession of faith" (Acts 8:12; 8:36-39; 16:33; 18:8). With the advent of the hymn of invitation that concludes many Baptist worship services, "walking the aisle" has become the "public profession of faith." Baptism, to some extent, has been made anticlimactic in contemporary Baptist life. But not in the New Testament and not in early Baptist life. The idea of Soul Freedom with its emphasis on the personal and voluntary nature of faith drove Baptists to adopt believers' baptism in order to have a believers' church.

In closing this brief study of the Baptist commitment to Soul Freedom, I commend to you two books that have been tragically overlooked by contemporary Baptists. They are excellent expositions of the concept of Soul Freedom and of Baptist distinctives in general. One is by Stewart A. Newman, long-time professor at both Southwestern Baptist Theological Seminary in Ft. Worth, Texas, and Southeastern Baptist Theological Seminary in Wake Forest, North Carolina. It is entitled *A Free Church Perspective: A Study in Ecclesiology.*

The second book was published in 1981 by Paulist Press for Roman Catholics, and it is entitled *Introducing Southern Baptists: Their Faith and Their Life.* This book was written by C. Brownlow Hastings, a life long Southern Baptist minister and long-time employee of the Home Mission Board of the Southern Baptist Convention. Hastings spent much of his career working to create better understanding between Southern Baptists and other religious groups. Precisely because this book is written to a non-Baptist audience, Hastings' explanations of who the Baptist people are and what they believe are simple, clear, and accurate.

What I have discussed in this present study as Soul Freedom, Hastings treats in his second chapter under the title of "The Competency of the Soul." He closes his chapter with sentences that illuminate the meaning of Soul Freedom:

> It is easy for us to yield our integrity and responsibility to some accepted authority: beloved pastor, honored teacher, influential book—even an edition of the Bible—respected parents or dynamic church. These all have their proper role of influence, but the final choice of belief and practice must be made in the secret of the soul's naked presence before God alone. I may pray in corporate prayer or use a devotional prayerbook, but unless their words are truly *my* words, I have not engaged God for myself. I have only "said my prayers." I may study the Bible under great teachers and share with devoted Christian friends, but I must finally judge what is truth, not because I find it agreeable to me, but because the inner witness of the Spirit convinces me. I may profit by the testimony of

another's experience in the Lord, but I do not need and cannot repeat his experience. I need my own. (Hastings, 24)

That is something of what is meant by the Baptist distinctive of Soul Freedom. The individual is central. The Christian faith is personal, experiential, and voluntary. Baptists really do believe that you have to "make up your own mind."

BIBLIOGRAPHY

Brackney, William Henry, *The Baptists*. New York: Greenwood Press, 1988.

Hastings, C. Brownlow, *Introducing Southern Baptists: Their Faith and Their Life*. New York: Paulist Press, 1981.

Mullins, E. Y., *The Axioms of Religion*. Philadelphia: American Baptist Publication Society, 1908.

Newman, Stewart A., *A Free Church Perspective: A Study in Ecclesiology*. Wake Forest, NC: Stevens Book Press, 1986.

Robinson, H. Wheeler, *Baptist Principles*. London: The Carey Kingsgate Press, 1925.

Stealey, Sydnor L., *A Baptist Treasury*. New York: Thomas Y. Crowell, 1958.

CHAPTER THREE

CHURCH FREEDOM

**CHURCH FREEDOM is the historic Baptist affirmation that
local churches are free, under the Lordship of Christ, to determine
their membership and leadership, to order their worship and
work, to ordain whom they perceive as gifted for ministry, male
or female, and to participate in the larger Body of Christ, of
whose unity and mission Baptists are proudly a part.**

INTRODUCTION

One of God's gifts to Baptists in the last half of the twentieth century
is a short Louisiana Frenchman by the name of Penrose St. Amant
(pronounced "San Amaw"). A former professor of church history at
New Orleans Baptist Theological Seminary and Southern Baptist
Theological Seminary, he also served brilliantly as Dean at Southern
and later as president at the International Baptist Theological Seminary in Ruschlikon, Switzerland. A respected scholar and a popular
preacher, an academic administrator and a superb classroom teacher,
an ecumenical churchman and a thoroughgoing Baptist, St. Amant
is a man of remarkable balance and stature who never forgot his roots.
In a moving, autobiographical passage, St. Amant described those
spiritual roots:

> My earliest memory of the church is a small congregation wor-
> shiping in a modest frame building in a predominantly Roman
> Catholic village in south Louisiana. The wooden, cushionless
> benches were always hard, the sermons often long, and my mother's

lap inviting. Often I went to sleep shortly after the sermon started and was usually awakened by the singing of a rousing gospel song. And yet what happened there was so meaningful that at the age of seven I made a public profession of faith in Christ, was baptized, and began to participate in the life of the church, a community of folk for whom Jesus Christ was Savior and Lord. Upon its deepest level, whatever else the church means, it still means this to me. (St. Amant, 88)

That paragraph is filled with words that say so much about the Baptist understanding of what the New Testament calls *ecclesia*. Note them carefully: "The church," "a small congregation," "worshiping," "sermons," "rousing gospel song," "meaningful," "public profession of faith," "baptized," and "participate." Also within this paragraph is an excellent Baptist definition of the church in highly non-theological language: "a community of folks for whom Jesus Christ was Savior and Lord."

The phrase "Church Freedom" is one way of understanding the Baptist concept of the church. Baptists belong to that part of Protestantism called the "Free Church Tradition." The expression has often been used to refer to Baptists and other groups in Europe who dissent from the Established Church in various countries. Baptists have certainly been "free" churches in that sense, but that is not the primary meaning of the phrase "Free Church Tradition."

As I argued in the last chapter, and as Stewart A. Newman insists, the Free Church Tradition affirms "the freedom and responsibility of the individual as being central in all matters of faith" (Newman, 3). This is not, however, spiritual lone rangerism. While the individual is central, the individual is always an "individual in community." Baptists do not understand the story line of the Bible as simply the heroic achievements of isolated individuals. Abraham, Moses, David, Jeremiah, Peter, and Paul are not pictured in the Bible as invincible individualists who, in their isolation, whipped the forces of evil. They are portrayed as people in community—Israel in the Old Testament and the Church in the New Testament—who are aware of historical identity and treasured traditions. They are in need of the genuine values of relationships. The dialectic of freedom and responsibility that informs the Baptist distinctives of religious authority and salvation, which we have already discussed, is also essential in understanding the Baptist concept of the church.

THE CHURCH:
FREE TO FOLLOW VOLUNTARILY

In his colloquial translation of the New Testament, Clarence Jordan, one of the preeminent white Baptist prophets of the South, translated "the kingdom of God" as "the God Movement." It may not be too far off the mark, as Stewart Newman suggests, to define the church as "the Jesus Crowd." The church is a people with a double promise, freely and voluntarily made. First, they have promised to follow Jesus as Lord of their lives. They have promised, secondly, to help each other struggle to follow Jesus as Lord. That dual pledge is referred to by Baptists as a covenant; individuals covenant with God and with each other to form a Baptist church.

One of Baptists' earliest concerns was the nature of the church. They came out of a culture where one was "born" into the church. To become a member of the church one did not make a conscious choice to follow Jesus as Lord. Rather, one was baptized in infancy and accepted into the church within the geographical "parish" of one's birth. In contrast to this concept of a "parish" church, built upon the ideas of infant baptism and the union of church and state, Baptists insisted on a "gathered church." A "gathered" church consisted of those who made self-conscious and voluntary decisions to confess Jesus as Lord of their lives.

Baptists have used other terms to communicate the idea that the church is "gathered" or, as St. Amant said, "a community of folk" for whom Jesus Christ is "Savior and Lord." They sometimes refer to this as the "pure church ideal," meaning that the church should always strive to have a membership composed only of those who sincerely want to be a part of the "Jesus Crowd." One may also hear Baptists speak of this as "regenerate" church membership. The church is restricted to those who have been "regenerated by God's Spirit" or "born again." Probably the term that Baptists have used most often to describe their concept of the church is that of a "Believers' Church." Because authentic faith is a matter of personal choice, the church should only include those persons who have deliberately committed themselves to the way of Christ.

The phrase "believers' church" is perfectly good language to communicate the Baptist notion. But one must not equate faith in Jesus with mere intellectual assent to doctrinal ideas. In their beginning and historically throughout the years, Baptists have been interested in far more than a nod of the head to a certain theology. Baptists want a personal commitment to the Jesus way of living. If "faith" does not mean "following," there is no "gathered" or "believers'" church. Baptism, therefore, is significant for Baptists not because it washes away sin or communicates grace but because it dramatizes the Christ-way of life, freely and deliberately chosen. Only believers, say Baptists, should be baptized.

Baptists have spoken of the church as both local and universal. The universal church is the Body of Christ that includes all the redeemed—all the followers—of all the ages. Jesus said, "I will build my church." His reference is clearly to his one people. The sublime theme of the book of Ephesians is God's eternal purpose in establishing and completing the universal church that includes both Jew and Gentile. Baptists have a theology of the church that encourages relationships with non-Baptist Christians. At their best, Baptists have acknowledged that the one Body of Christ does not begin or end with their denomination or with a local Baptist church.

Baptists have spent most of their time, however, speaking of the church in a local sense. That the New Testament is replete with this emphasis is fruitless to debate (1 Cor 1:2; Rom 1:7; 1 Thess 1:1). The church is local. It meets in flesh and blood at 511 High Place and at 2100 Monument Boulevard and at your local church's address. It is in terms of the local church that Baptists have argued for the freedom of self-government, the freedom of worship style, and the freedom to carry out its ministry to Jesus Christ.

THE CHURCH:
FREE TO GOVERN OBEDIENTLY

For Baptists, Church Freedom means that a local Baptist Church has the right and responsibility to run its own affairs under the Lordship of Jesus Christ. No bishop or pastor, no civil leader or magistrate, no religious body or convention of churches can dictate to the local church. To permit such dictation is to abdicate freedom and obligation. Idealistically, Baptists want the local church to be a Christocracy. They want the Jesus Crowd to be obedient to the will and mind of Christ. Practically, Baptists settle for a democracy. To say it another way, Baptists hope to implement the rule of Christ through the mechanism of the full participation of the congregation.

Baptists follow, therefore, what is called congregational church government. Among Christian denominations one finds three basic types of church government. They are episcopal, presbyterian, and congregational. In episcopal church government, authority is placed in the hands of one person, usually a bishop. In presbyterian church government, authority is vested in a small group, often called elders within the local church. In congregational church government, authority is placed in the hands of all the members of the church. This is sometimes facetiously referred to as mobocracy!

A honest reading of the New Testament compels one to say that the details of church polity are not spelled out there. Texts from various parts of the New Testament may be called upon to support all three types of church government. If, however, one affirms the Free Church Tradition where the individual is central, one may easily accept congregationalism as the most theologically appropriate approach to government.

Baptists practice democratic church polity not because it is more efficient or more reliable or even more biblical than other forms. They follow it because it accents the role of the individual within community, allowing the greatest freedom for the greatest number of people to have a say. Moreover, democratic church polity is a statement of the equality of all believers in determining the mind of Christ. Baptists would like to think that it provides more freedom for the Holy Spirit to guide the life of the local church. Even here, however, Baptists have never equated the voice of the majority with the voice of God.

Congregational church government mandates that a local church determine its own membership, decide its own pattern of worship, map its own mission strategy, and elect its own officers. Baptist churches have two offices, ministers and deacons. Ministers in a Baptist church include those who serve in special areas of music, education, youth, children, counseling, as well as the pastor. Deacons are laypeople called to serve with the ministers on behalf of the congregation. A congregation may call whomever it wishes, women or men, to serve as ministers or deacons.

Threats always exist to congregational church government. Maybe the most perennial threat is the passivity of the believers themselves. Local churches can simply "go along" with what other churches are doing or saying or believing and refuse to take responsibility for their life together. This is to fall prey to a crippling conformity that is diametrically opposed to the spirit of freedom and dissent in the Baptist tradition.

But congregationalism is also endangered by the activity of authoritarians. A few summers ago I spoke to a meeting of associational directors of missions from across the Southern Baptist Convention. I asked them, "What is the major issue you face in the churches of your association?" The issue they identified was pastoral authoritarianism. A hierarchy, whether in Roman Catholicism or Protestantism, destroys congregationalism and the historic Baptist idea of the equality of believers in the local church.

Congregationalism never meant isolationism of Baptist churches from one another. Within less than fifty years of the formation of the first Baptist church in the seventeenth century, Baptist churches voluntarily began grouping themselves into "associations." They did this for both theological reasons, to show their oneness in Christ, and practical reasons, to strengthen their witness in the world. Later Baptists formed "conventions," "unions," and "General Assemblies," units of regional or national organization that unified their work beyond the local and associational levels.

One should note, however, that the organizations beyond the local church do not together with the local churches constitute *"The* Baptist Church."* There is no *"The* Baptist Church" in the same sense that there is *"The* Presbyterian Church" or *"The* Methodist Church." Such terminology suggests a centralization and authority of the various ecclesiastical units that is not allowed by Baptist congregationalism.

No organization exists in Baptist life that is superior to or legislates for local Baptist churches. It is, therefore, theologically incorrect to speak of *"The* Southern Baptist Church," or *"The* Progressive National Baptist Church," or *"The* American Baptist Church." Rather, one speaks of "The Southern Baptist Convention (of churches)" or "The Progressive National Baptist Convention (of churches)" or "The American Baptist Churches, U.S.A." This is important because occasionally one hears someone erroneously say something such as, "Well, The Southern Baptist Church believes thus and so about this or that." A group of Southern Baptists can meet and pass resolutions or motions on any issue they wish, but they do not, thereby, commit local Southern Baptist churches to that point of view.

So the Baptist understanding of the church, while rooted in congregationalism, does not preclude cooperation with other Baptist churches in associations, societies, conventions, unions, or General Assemblies. Moreover, as suggested earlier, the Baptist notion of ecclesiology (the study of the church), does not by any means preclude interdenominational or ecumenical activities by Baptists. There is no aspect of the Baptist concept of the church that automatically keeps Baptists separate from organizations such as the National Council of Churches or the World Council of Churches, any more than it keeps them apart from the Baptist World Alliance.

British Baptists, American Baptists, and some of the African American Baptist groups have a long and valuable ecumenical connection. While the largest part of the Baptist family, the Southern Baptist Convention, has not historically identified with the National Council or World Council, nothing in their ecclesiology forbids it. Baptists need to hear what their sisters and brothers of other Christian communions have to say. Likewise, Baptists have *something* to say themselves. All Baptists groups, therefore, would be wise to break out of their self-imposed isolation from other Christian groups and enter into ecumenical dialogue and action.

THE CHURCH:
FREE TO WORSHIP CREATIVELY

No two Baptist churches are exactly alike. Although they have similar programs, schedules, staff, facilities, and polity, the uniqueness of each congregation is striking. These differences engender potential for creative ministries (Rom 12:6-8). Baptist churches often affirm and acknowledge this diversity that is rooted in congregational church government. This diversity manifests itself as clearly in various styles of worship as anywhere in Baptist life.

When Baptists began in seventeenth-century England, a crucial part of their cry for freedom was the determination to worship God according to conscience. Specifically, they wanted freedom from the set forms of Anglicanism as recorded in *The Book of Common Prayer.* Their aim was to personalize and revitalize worship.

The Baptist attitude for free worship is often incorrectly referred to as anti-liturgical. But if liturgy is interpreted as "the work of the people," the original meaning of the word, Baptists are not anti-liturgical at all. If, however, liturgy means prescribed and imposed forms, Baptists are most certainly anti-liturgical.

Historically, Baptists have been concerned with emptiness in worship. What they have been wary of are impersonal and mechanical features in worship. But many Baptist churches recognize that worship may be exceedingly informal and at the same time highly impersonal, rote, and stuck in a deadly routine that lacks vitality. Informality does not necessarily equal vitality. To the contrary, worship may be quite formal, with robes for the minister as well as for the choir, beautifully written and read prayers, powerfully read sermons, beautiful affirmations of faith, congregational litanies, and the use of classical Christian music and be spiritually reviving for believers.

The Baptist freedom for worship aims at an authentic spiritual offering being presented to God. But Baptist worship does not dictate *how* worship is to be structured. Indeed, just as Bible Freedom offers individuals the right of private interpretation of the Bible and just as Soul Freedom issues into different types of personal conversion, Church Freedom results in different forms of worship, some of which are surprisingly formal and some exceedingly informal.

Whatever form the worship of a local Baptist congregation takes, it is an act of the entire believing community and not the separate performances of the presiding ministers. Public worship in the Free Church Tradition is not a spectator's sport. Unlike some groups, Baptists do not go to worship "to take communion" from the minister. Neither should Baptists go simply "to attend preaching," which they have done far too often. Too much of Baptist corporate worship is evaluated only in terms of the brilliance of the sermon or the inspiration of the choir.

The Baptist doctrine of the priesthood of believers needs to be incorporated more extensively into the worshiping life of Baptist churches. This calls for extensive congregational participation. The use of congregational calls to worship, congregational prayers, (especially the Lord's Prayer), congregational responsive readings, congregational quotation of scripture, and congregational singing are ways to accomplish this participation. Even the word "Amen" is not primarily a convenient way to conclude a prayer. It means "so be it" and provides an opportunity for the whole worshipping community to affirm what has been said. "Amen" is a word that belongs to the people.

Baptists recognize baptism and the Lord's Supper as the two New Testament ordinances. Baptists call them ordinances because they believe they were ordained by Christ himself (Matt 28: 19-20; 1 Cor 11:24-25). While many Baptists, maybe most, are reluctant to refer to baptism and the Lord's Supper as "sacraments," this is not universally so. British Baptists, among others, speak of both as "sacraments" and as "means of grace" (as cited in Payne, 288). One may find the same among some Baptists of North America.

For believers only, these two ordinances may be administered by any believer authorized by the local church. Baptist baptism is by immersion because it symbolizes the death, burial, and resurrection of the believer with Christ (Rom 6:3-4). While immersion is the universal practice of Baptists, some Baptist churches accept other Christians into their fellowship if they have received believers' baptism by any mode. Indeed, some Baptist churches accept other Christians into their membership without regard to believers' baptism or immersion. These churches are primarily concerned with whether the new member is indeed a believer. If so, and the person is satisfied with his or her baptism, the person is received into the fellowship.

The Lord's Supper portrays God's love for us, our communion with him, and our communion with other believers. Usually celebrated monthly, the frequency of observance is by no means uniform in Baptist churches. Most, but not all, Baptist churches today practice "open" communion, inviting all Christians of whatever denomination to the table of the Lord.

THE CHURCH:
FREE TO MINISTER RESPONSIBLY

The Baptist concept of Church Freedom also means that the ministry of the church is open to all classes of people and specific mission strategies. Although the Southern Baptist Convention derided and misunderstood the doctrine of the priesthood of all believers in official convention action in 1988, Southern Baptists, as all other Baptists, have historically stood solidly for the concept that the ministry belongs to the laity of the church. Every believer is on equal footing with every other believer in the local Baptist church. No pastor has official or constituted authority to "rule over" anybody in a Baptist congregation. Why? Because all Christians are priests before God. As such, all Christians have the freedom and the responsibility to minister in the name of Christ.

Likewise, believers in a local Baptist church are saddled with the freedom and responsibility of deciding how the church will witness for Christ in their local community. Baptist Church Freedom was never intended as an exercise in selfishness. Early Baptists did not insist on freedom just so their faith could be a private possession.

Either the gospel drives us outside ourselves and outside the fellowship of the church into a world God loves or else the gospel has not captured our lives. Christians are not catch basins but conduits of God's grace and compassion. God is interested in more than our personal salvation or the growth of our local churches. God is interested in shaping people's lives through God's people.

The mission of the church has been interpreted in various ways in Baptist history. William Carey aroused Baptists to world missions in 1792. Luther Rice and Adoniram Judson, inspired by Carey, did the same thing for Baptists in America. Missionary outreach has been part of the heartbeat of Baptists since Carey's time. Billy Graham, more than any other one person, has embodied the Baptist interest in personal evangelism during the last half of the twentieth century.

While missions and evangelism have been a major part of the Baptist mission, Baptists have not been without a witness in issues of social justice. John Clifford and Walter Rauschenbusch, both individualistic Baptists, saw the relationship of a personal gospel to the issues of society. Martin Luther King, Jr. saw the mission of Baptist churches, indeed of all churches, to be cheerleaders for justice and equality. Much of the best and most creative work of the Baptist World Alliance has been in the area of world hunger and related social areas.

Baptists believe in "gathered" churches. At their best Baptists have also been "going" and "caring" churches. Dietrich Bonhoeffer, a Lutheran who died as a martyr under Hitler, has inspired many contemporary Baptists. Eberhard Bethge, a close friend of Bonhoeffer, wrote the standard biography of Bonhoeffer. In an interview Bethge was asked what he thought Bonhoeffer would be saying to the church today. Bethge answered: "At the end Bonhoeffer saw in his experience . . .that the church, with its dominating statue in the Western world, must now step down below" (as cited in Hunter and Johnson, 141).

Of Jesus it was said, "He . . . emptied himself, taking the form of a slave" (Phil 2:7). "The church . . . must now step down below." How does the church become a servant? That is the question Baptists have insisted that the church must be free to ask and answer.

How does the church "step down" in your local setting? Local Baptist churches cannot allow others to tell them how to become a servant of Christ. A local Baptist church is free to design its own servant ministry. Moreover, it is responsible for doing so.

BIBLIOGRAPHY

Hunter, Victor L. and Phillip Johnson. *The Human Church in the Presence of Christ.* Macon: Mercer University Press, 1985.

Newman, Stewart A. *A Free Church Perspective: A Study in Ecclesiology.* Wake Forest, NC: Stevens Book Press, 1986.

St. Amant, Penrose, "Our Baptist Heritage and the Church," *Baptist History and Heritage* 2:2 (July 1967): 83.

CHAPTER FOUR

RELIGIOUS FREEDOM

RELIGIOUS FREEDOM is the historic Baptist affirmation of freedom *OF* religion, freedom *FOR* religion, and freedom *FROM* religion, insisting that Caesar is not Christ and Christ is not Caesar.

INTRODUCTION

Historically, the relationship between church and state has been difficult, at times tortuous. Even scripture proposes diverse interpretations of this relationship. In Matthew 22:15-22, Jesus recognizes both the legitimacy and limitations of the state. In Romans 13:1-7, Paul accents the legitimacy of the state because Christians were not in danger from the state. In Revelation 13, however, during a time of persecution, John advocates resistance to the state to the point of martyrdom.

No one model fits all circumstances and epochs of history. Baptist Christians have acknowledged the diversity of biblical teaching on the relation of the church to the state. Often they have been "Romans 13 People," appreciative of civil government. Occasionally they have been "Revelation 13 People," opposing the state with their very lives. Most of the time, however, they have been "Matthew 22 People," legitimizing but limiting the state. In their persistent call for religious freedom and the separation of church and state, however, Baptists have been consistent. Yet, today, the Baptist position on religious freedom is under attack.

Nothing is more difficult than trying to arouse people to action when they do not see the need for action. But William R. Estep has made the effort. In a magnificent book entitled *Revolution Within The Revolution,* Estep, the former Distinguished Professor of Church History at Southwestern Baptist Theological Seminary, makes the distressing charge that the First Amendment of the Constitution of the United States is currently "under siege." That amendment reads: "Congress shall make no law respecting an establishment of religion, or prohibiting the free exercise thereof."

This cherished statement, which Baptists of the eighteenth century insisted upon, is now "under siege" says Estep, by, of all people, some Christians! Misguided but extremely dangerous, these people want to eliminate the First Amendment either by constitutional convention or by reinterpretation. This current situation is "nothing less than a crisis of faith in freedom itself," screams Estep.

But for Baptists who believe in the historic principles of religious freedom, here is the really devastating charge from Estep. SOME PROMINENT BAPTIST PREACHERS HAVE JOINED THE SIEGE AGAINST THE FIRST AMENDMENT! He quotes one of them who said on national television: "I believe the notion of separation of church and state was the figment of some infidel's imagination." Charging with one hundred percent accuracy that this attitude represents "a radical break" with Baptists' historical commitment to separation of church and state, Estep believes that some current Baptists suffer from an "identity crisis" (Estep, 9).

Estep, a man who has spent his life studying the Baptist heritage, says some current Baptists do not know who Baptists really are. Well, who are they? Particularly, who are Baptists when it comes to the issue of religious freedom? What have they really said and done? Why did they say and do it? What did they mean by what they said and did? What are the threats to religious liberty in contemporary America and how should Baptists, in light of their heritage, respond to those threats?

HISTORIC BAPTISTS AND THE WITNESS TO RELIGIOUS FREEDOM

Preaching the keynote address before the opening session of the Baptist World Alliance in London, England, in 1905, John D. Freeman, one of Canadian Baptists most celebrated pastors at that time and later professor at Mercer University, chose as his subject, "The Place of Baptists in the Christian Church." Claiming that the essential Baptist principle is the personal, direct, and undelegated authority of Jesus Christ over the souls of people, Freeman said that the concept carried with it "the *radical and far-reaching Baptist doctrine of individualism.*" It was the doctrine of individualism, said Freeman, that made Baptists the champions of religious liberty. And of the doctrine of religious liberty he said, "We did not stumble upon the doctrine. It inheres (exists) in the very essence of our belief."

Freeman was absolutely correct. Baptists did not "stumble" on the idea of religious liberty. John Smyth and Thomas Helwys, trailblazers of the Baptist tradition in early seventeenth-century England, launched the Baptist denomination with no uncertain sound on issues of liberty. Smyth's hand is behind the "the first confession of faith of modern times to demand freedom of conscience and separation of church and state" (Lumpkin, 124).

In 1612 Helwys, a layman, wrote *A Short Declaration of the Mistery of Iniquity.* Many historians say that it is the first plea for complete religious freedom in the English language. Brashly he inscribed a handwritten note, sent a copy to King James I, and kindly reminded him that "the king is a mortal man and not God" and "therefore has no power over the immortal souls of his subjects."

Within the document itself, Helwys affirmed loyalty to the state, the limitations of the state, and the principle of religious liberty for all people. "Let them be heretics, Turks, Jews, or whatsoever, it appertaines not to the earthly power to punish them in the least measure" (as cited in Estep, 53). And why should the powers of state keep their hands off of folks' souls? Helwys gave the same reason in 1612 that Freeman gave almost three hundred years later, in 1905. Because, in Helwys' words, "mens religion to God is betwixt God and themselves." The doctrine of full religious liberty, now taken for granted, was a perilous and heretical concept then. Helwys paid. Promptly thrown into prison, he died there in 1616.

Also in the seventeenth century, but on the other side of the ocean, Roger Williams, John Clarke, and Obadiah Holmes clamored in the colonies for unrestricted religious liberty. Isaac Backus and John Leland took up the chorus in the eighteenth and early nineteenth centuries. By the fourth decade of the nineteenth century in America, the last state church had ceased to exist. No religious denomination did more to accomplish that reality than the Baptists.

Throughout the twentieth century troubled Baptist voices—such as E. Y. Mullins, Rufus Weaver, J.M. Dawson, George W. Truett, James E. Wood, Jr., G. Hugh Wamble, and James M. Dunn—have implored Baptists not to forget the Baptist witness to liberty *for all*. That message is much easier to hear and act upon when you are small and powerless. When a denomination gets large and powerful and courted for political reasons, the bells of freedom ring fainter and flatter.

HISTORIC BAPTISTS AND THE FOUNDATIONS OF RELIGIOUS FREEDOM

On what do Baptists rest their case regarding freedom of conscience? It is a relatively modern and bold conviction to affirm that people should be able to believe without coercion, to practice their faith without constraint, and to spread their faith without hindrance. How have Baptists and others justified that conviction?

Throughout Christian history, the Bible has been used in contradictory ways to support both religious liberty and persecution. For example, some have used the parable of the Great Banquet in Luke 14:15-24 as a justification for force in Christianity. After all, did not the master say to the servants, "Go out into the roads and lanes, and *compel* them to come in, so that my house may be filled." After the wedding of Christianity to the Roman Empire by Constantine in the fourth century, some discovered that force would work in increasing the size of the church. This text often became the biblical license for force. Others, however, used the parable of the Tares and the Wheat in Matthew 13:24-30 to defend religious liberty. "Let both of them grow together until the harvest . . ." is the counter text to "compel them to come in."

The misuse and abuse of these specific parables is obvious. Rather than basing their commitments to religious liberty on specific texts, Baptists have been more inclined to build on biblical principles. Religious freedom could be based on the ancient idea of human reason and the need for a society of equals to concede to one another the right of free discussion. But neither has this been the primary appeal of Baptists.

They have anchored their passion for religious liberty to (1) the nature of God, (2) the nature of humanity, and (3) the nature of faith. First, religious freedom is rooted in the very nature of God. A sovereign God who dared to create us as free beings is portrayed in the Bible as a liberating Deity. Throughout the Old Testament, God is set against persons and institutions that restricted the freedom of people. And the complete thrust of Jesus' ministry was to free people from all that would hold them back from fulfilling their potential under God. Freedom is more than a constitutional right or a governmental gift. God, not nations or courts or human law, is the ultimate source of liberty. That is the theological pillar on which Baptists set their love of freedom.

As was noted in the study on Soul Freedom, Religious Liberty is also based on the biblical view of persons. Created in the image of God, a human being is the crowning work of God's creation (Ps 8). Human personality is sacred and life's highest value. To deny freedom of conscience to any person is to debase God's creation.

Religious liberty, therefore, is founded on the nature of God and on the biblical view of persons. Baptists have also argued for religious freedom from the biblical nature of faith. To be authentic, faith must be free. Genuine faith cannot be forced or denied by the state.

HISTORIC BAPTISTS AND THE MEANING OF RELIGIOUS FREEDOM

In the Baptist heritage, religious freedom has several dimensions. First, freedom of religion represents a commitment to complete religious liberty and not simply religious toleration. Religious liberty and religious toleration are not the same. Religious toleration is a concession; religious liberty is a right. Religious toleration is a measure of expediency; religious liberty is a matter of principle.

Second, historically Baptists have been clear that religious liberty is for all, not for a selected few nor even for an overwhelming majority. The Baptist insistence on freedom *of* religion includes, therefore, freedom *from* religion. One's right not to believe is as sacred as one's right to believe. Those Baptists of the 1990s would do well to go back and read another Baptist of the 1790s. John Leland wrote in 1791 a document entitled "The Rights of Conscience Inalienable," in which he said that "Government has no more to do with the religious opinions of men, than it has with the principles of mathematics." Then Leland called for absolute religious liberty:

> Let every man speak freely without fear, maintain the principles that he believes, worship according to his own faith, either one God, three Gods, no God, or twenty Gods; and let government protect him in so doing. (Leland, 184)

But Leland's was no eccentric Baptist voice in this regard. Helwys called for the precise same universal liberty in 1612. And E. Y. Mullins, in 1923, said,

> Baptists believe in religious liberty for themselves. But they believe in it equally for all men. With them it is not only a right; it is also a passion. While we have no sympathy with atheism or agnosticism or materialism, we stand for the freedom of the atheist, agnostic, and materialist in his religious or irreligious convictions. (as cited in Shurden, 62)

George W. Truett, former pastor of the First Baptist Church in Dallas, Texas, echoed this historic Baptist position of religious liberty for all when he said,

> Baptists make this contention, not only for themselves, but as well, for all others—for Protestants of all denominations, for Romanists, for Jews, for Quakers, for Turks, for Pagans, for all men everywhere. (as cited in Shurden, 115)

Third, religious freedom means separation of church and state and not accommodation of church with state. Four patterns of church-state relations are evident in Christian history and the contemporary world. The first is that of church *above* state, present through much of the medieval era. The second is church *under* state, manifest in the twentieth century in communist countries. The third is the accommodation of a particular church *with* the state; the most prominent example is the Anglican Church in England. Freedom of expression is given to all, but preferential treatment given to one. The fourth form of church-state relationship is the separation of church and state, the American model. This is better expressed as "a free church in a free state" or church and state *side by side*. Baptists, not only in America, but around the world have been solidly on the side of the separation of church and state.

BAPTISTS TODAY AND THREATS TO RELIGIOUS FREEDOM

A major threat to religious freedom today, as Glenn Hinson reminded back in 1975, is that Baptists will "assume that there is no danger" or that "the danger is too slight to bother" (Hinson, 122). Baptists today are not whipped on the streets as was Obadiah Holmes in seventeenth-century Boston or jailed as were those preachers in colonial America. If you think, however, that the danger is too slight to bother, go quickly to a bookstore and purchase Estep's book mentioned at the beginning of this chapter. Worth the price of the book are the "Foreword" by Bill Moyers and the first chapter in which Estep highlights chilling contemporary threats to the First Amendment.

If that does not sufficiently alarm you, listen to Chief Justice William Rehnquist of the Supreme Court of the United States of America when he says, "The 'wall of separation between church and state' is a metaphor based on bad history, a metaphor that has proved useless as a guide to judging. It should be frankly and explicitly abandoned" *(Church and State,* April 1990, 24). Whatever the Chief Justice meant, it does not bode well for the historic Baptist principle of religious freedom and separation of church and state.

The danger of undermining this historic principle is real even within Baptist life. During a television interview in 1984, Pastor W. A. Criswell, senior minister of the largest church in the Southern Baptist Convention, understandably alarmed many of his viewers when he said, "I believe this notion of the separation of church and state was the figment of some infidel's imagination." Note how far Criswell's statement deviates from that of his predecessor, Dr. George W. Truett. Preaching from the east steps of the National Capitol Building on May 16, 1920, Truett said that Jesus' word about rendering unto Caesar what is Caesar's and unto God what is God's was one of the "most revolutionary and history making utterances that ever fell from those lips divine." "That utterance," Truett said, "once for all, marked the divorcement of church and state." He spoke of the need for the doctrine of "a free church in a free state" to have universal acceptance (as cited in McBeth, 471).

Another serious threat to the principle of religious freedom is the theocratic mind-set of some Christians involved in what is known as the Reconstruction Movement. A small but growing movement that is popular within fundamentalist circles, this group seeks to restructure American society on the basis of the Old Testament. R. J. Rushdoony and Gary North, ardent Calvinists, spearhead this movement that would replace American democracy with a Christian theocracy. "If the advocates of this radical reordering of American society have their way," says William Estep, "religious freedom will vanish" (Estep, 12).

Another danger, more popular and subtle, is the confusion of citizenship and discipleship. Sometimes referred to as "Civil Religion," this attitude calls for, among other things, prayer in public schools, the channeling of public tax dollars into the support of private religious programs, and the presence of religious symbols in civil contexts. Christians have to work hard at distinguishing between pietism and patriotism, assessing critically where one begins and the other ends. When the cross of Jesus is wrapped in the flag of any nation, danger, if not downright heresy, is close by.

Nationalism is not the faith of Christians. Baptists especially have insisted that the state is always subordinate to the Lordship of Jesus Christ. There are indications in the last several years that the lines of church and state are becoming seriously blurred in America, even among some Baptists.

It is easy for a people—even Baptist people—to call for religious liberty when they do not have it. It is easy for a people—even Baptist people—to call for separation of church and state when the union of church and state limits their freedoms. It is easy for a people—even Baptist people—to distinguish between discipleship and citizenship when Caesar is less than friendly. Throughout the seventeenth, eighteenth, and early nineteenth centuries, such were the Baptist circumstances. During those years, Baptists pled for religious liberty and the separation of church and state on the basis of principle. This was not simply self-serving expediency; it was **principle**! And it was a principle applied to **all** people. Baptists were also clear in those early years about what they called "the crown rights of the Redeemer"—the idea that Christ wields ultimate authority in the life of the believer and that allegiance to Christ is never to be confused with the partisan claims of patriotism.

But what now? What about Baptists today? Having become prominent and powerful, especially in the United States, are we still as committed to religious liberty for all persons as our ancestors were? And does this include those outside the Judeo-Christian tradition? Does it include those outside **any** religious tradition? Do we believe in separation of church and state as much today when it benefits us as we did in a day when it worked against us? Baptists are now one of the most powerful religious groups in the most powerful nation in the world. Power can corrupt and blind us to our heritage. Power, however, in defense of the principle of religious liberty, can work to the vitality of the church and the good of the republic.

BIBLIOGRAPHY

Estep, William R., *Revolution Within The Revolution: The First Amendment in Historical Context, 1612–1789.* Grand Rapids, Michigan: William B. Eerdmans Publishing Company, 1990.

Greene, L. F., *The Writings of John Leland.* New York: Arno Press, 1969. Reprinted from the 1845 edition.

Hinson, E. Glenn, *Soul Liberty: The Doctrine of Religious Liberty.* Nashville: Convention Press, 1975.

Lumpkin, William L., *Baptist Confessions of Faith.* Valley Forge: The Judson Press, 1959.

McBeth, H. Leon, *A Sourcebook for Baptist Heritage.* Nashville: Broadman Press, 1990.

Shurden, Walter B., editor, *The Life of Baptists in the Life of the World.* Nashville: Broadman Press, 1985.

SUMMARY AND CONCLUSIONS

Standing near the end of the twentieth century, I agree completely with John D. Freeman, who said at the first meeting of the Baptist World Alliance, near the beginning of the twentieth century,

> The world has not outgrown the need of Baptist principles. It was never in greater need of them than it is to-day. Our principles have not yet manifested the full force that is in them. New light and power are to break forth from them in the days to come. Loose them and let them go (as cited in Shurden, 28–29).

If Baptists experienced a rebirth of commitment to Bible Freedom, Soul Freedom, Church Freedom, and Religious Freedom, they would not only rediscover their roots and their identity, they would become prophetically relevant to the world today.

Fortunately we are not limited to one word that summarizes the Baptist identity, but I am convinced that the one word that comes closer than any other to capturing the historic Baptist identity is the word "freedom." This is a strange assertion at a time when many view Baptists as narrow, provincial, and even reactionary.

Walker Percy, one of the great American novelists of the last half of the twentieth century, represents many with his portrayal of Baptists. In one of his novels he has a character say that "if heaven is full of Southern Baptists, I'd rather rot in hell with Saladin and Achilles" *(Lancelot,* 176). In other places Percy portrays Baptists as a group of evangelistically repulsive *(The Second Coming,* 218), anti-Catholics *(Love In the Ruins,* 22), who are political opportunists advocating scientific creationism *(The Thanatos Syndrome,* 347).

One need not believe that Percy is accurate to concede that he is describing what many assume the Baptist identity to be. My point is that Baptists are not perceived as freedom-lovers and freedom-givers by many persons outside the Baptist community. The essential and historic liberal spirit of freedom-devoted Baptists is not known or acknowledged today.

All of that notwithstanding, I would still contend that the historic essence of the Baptist spirit—what historian Martin Marty called "Baptistification"—is the voluntary approach to life and faith. This freedom is not tangential to the Baptist identity; it is at the core of what it means to be a Baptist. This voluntariness and freedom manifests itself in every area of the Christian life—in salvation (Soul Freedom), in religious authority (Bible Freedom), in church life (Church Freedom), and in civic life (Religious Freedom).

While contending that freedom is basic to understanding the Baptist identity, I must also insist that Baptist freedom, like all freedom, is very, very fragile. The sub-title of this book is important. Baptist freedoms are fragile; they are too readily relinquished from within and too easily pirated from without. Freedom can be abdicated. Freedom can also be stolen. Freedom-lovers have no choice but to be vigilant in the defense of freedom. Doubtless, this is why the Southern Baptist authors of the statement on "Baptist Ideals" warned in 1964 that "forces in the world" and "trends in our churches and in our denomination" endanger the Baptist identity.

Freedom is often undermined by irresponsibility. That is why I have tried to underscore that for every Baptist freedom there is a corresponding responsibility. Bible freedom is undermined by the irresponsibility of failing to study the Bible diligently with an open mind and a reverent spirit. It is undermined by falling into a blind subjectivism that ignores the Christian tradition and community and has nothing to fall back on in interpretation but "Well, this is what it means to me." And it is undermined by abdicating the struggle of personal interpretation to outside authorities. Above all, Bible freedom is undermined when one fails to bring one's life under the control and direction of scripture.

Soul Freedom or "soul competency" is simply another way of stressing "individual responsibility" for moral and religious decision making. Where there is no freedom or responsibility to choose faith, there is no **authentic** faith. And to choose faith in Christ is to confess that one intends to obey, to be responsible in light of the life and spirit of Christ.

Within the concept of Church Freedom, or what Baptists have historically called "the gathered church," lies "the profound conviction of the importance of each Christian's growth to spiritual maturity and of the responsibility which, as a member of the divine family, she or he should constantly exercise" (Appendix V). Baptist democracy calls for free and responsible participation in church life. Moreover, Baptist churches are, in the words of the Zagreb Statement, "free . . . and . . . duty bound" to enter into covenant with other Christians, both locally, nationally, and internationally (Appendix I).

Religious Freedom, too, has built-in responsibilities. While the state owes religion protection and full freedom, religion does not get a free ride. Maybe no statement on the Baptist identity made this responsibility clearer than did "Baptist Ideals." It said:

The church owes the state moral and spiritual reinforcement for law and order and the clear proclamation of those truths which undergird justice and peace. The church is responsible both to pray for the state and to declare the judgments of God as they relate to government, responsible citizenship, and the rights of all persons. The church must take seriously and practice consistently the principles which it declares should govern the relation of church and state. (Appendix VII)

This emphasis on Baptist freedom, for which I have argued, will sound strange to those who perceive Baptists as did Walker Percy. This emphasis on Baptist freedom should sound challenging to those who want to embrace the idea of freedom as the essential Baptist identity. But this emphasis on freedom will sound threatening to those who are more comfortable with control than with choice and who are more at home with uniformity than with diversity.

Freedom is always a dangerous and threatening idea. Soul Freedom, experiential and individualistic by nature, is threatening to both sacramental and rationalistic understandings of the Christian concept of salvation. Bible Freedom is threatening; that is why the Bible was chained to the pulpit in medieval times and why some seek to impose their biblical interpretations in modern times. Church Freedom is threatening to ecclesiastical authoritarians and political totalitarians. Religious Freedom is threatening to those who want to shape society into their own image and then mandate it through legislation for others.

To stress freedom is not to minimize faith. It is to say that marginal issues of faith such as "inerrancy" of scripture, the premillennial return of Christ, closed communion, and alien immersion are minimized. Indeed, what Baptists need to recover the most is the one element of their faith that holds all their freedoms together—the centrality of Christ and His Lordship over the Bible, our individual lives, our churches, and our relationship to the world, including the government. To confess the Lordship of Jesus Christ is no marginal or minimal confession; it is the core confession of the Baptist movement as the documents in these appendixes will attest.

It is no accident that the statement on "Baptist Distinctives and Diversity" begins with the affirmation that "the foundation truth upon which Baptists build is the Lordship of Christ over the individual believer" (Appendix II). It continues with specificity:

> All other authorities are judged by the authority of the son of God. Ultimate loyalty, therefore, is given to a Person, rather than to creeds, books, historic patterns, or effective procedures. Christ's will is mandatory for the believer.

As Christ becomes Lord and central in our lives, the Bible is given its appropriate place under his Lordship. While not being shoved to the side by tradition or made into a divine icon by established power, the Bible becomes our major avenue to the mind and the spirit of Christ. As the Zagreb Statement says, Baptists "start with the Scriptures" because they afford us God's self-revelation "supremely in the life, death and resurrection of Christ" (Appendix I).

As Christ becomes central, we will reaffirm without uniforming the evangelical experience that is at the heart of the Baptist faith— what English Baptists called "a personal crisis in the soul's life"

(Appendix V). Christ is Lord of the Believer; Christ is Lord over the Scriptures. Christ is also Lord of the church. "Under the Lordship of Christ and before the open Scriptures," says the Zagreb Statement of the local church, "it is competent, when properly summoned, in church meeting to govern itself, to determine a strategy for mission in its locality, and to appoint its minister (deacons and pastors) and other officers" (Appendix I). So with the state, Christ, not the powers of this world, is Lord of conscience. What I am saying at some length, American Baptists said succinctly: "That the freedom to respond to the Lordship of Christ in all circumstances is fundamental to the Christian Gospel and to human dignity" (Appendix VIII).

While confessing the risks and even the limitations of freedom within their central commitment to Christ as Lord, Baptists, when at their best, have nonetheless pursued freedom passionately. And they have done so because they rightly sense that there are forces inherent in life that would gladly jettison freedom. The historical Baptist identity, therefore, has been chiseled primarily from freedom rather than control, voluntaryism rather than coercion, individualism rather than a "pack mentality," personal religion rather than proxy religion, and diversity rather than uniformity.

BIBLIOGRAPHY

Shurden, Walter B., editor. *The Life of Baptists in the Life of the World.* Nashville: Broadman Press, 1985.

Percy, Walker. *Lancelot.* New York: Farrar, Straus and Giroux, 1977.

Percy, Walker. *Love in the Ruins.* New York: Avon Books, 1971.

Percy, Walker. *The Second Coming.* New York: Washington Square Press, 1980.

Percy, Walker. *The Thanatos Syndrome.* New York: Farrar, Straus, and Giroux, 1987.

DOCUMENTS ON THE BAPTIST IDENTITY

Baptists are fortunate to have several good collections of their important denominational documents, some of which I have depended on and alluded to in the previous chapters and listed in the bibliography. These include the collections of Baptist confessions of faith by McGlothlin, Lumpkin, and Parker, and the general collections of Baptist resources by Stealey and McBeth. Three sources that I did not cite but are also very helpful are Charles W. Deweese, *Baptist Church Covenants* (Broadman), Robert A. Baker, *A Baptist Source Book* (Broadman), and William H. Brackney, *Baptist Life and Thought: 1600–1980* (Judson Press).

What follows are some twentieth-century documents on the Baptist identity. They are printed here for various reasons. Some, like "Towards A Baptist Identity," "A Pronouncement Upon Religious Liberty," and "Baptist Distinctives and Diversities," are included because they represent more than one tradition of Baptists and may, therefore, be of the greatest importance in describing the Baptist identity without the intrusion of regional, racial, theological, or ethnic characteristics. Even the statement, "The Baptist Doctrine of the Church," while originating in England and certainly having the definite stamp of British Baptists on it, is broadly representative of the worldwide Baptist position.

Two others are printed simply because they are relatively new documents and have not had broad circulation in the Baptist community beyond their own constituencies. These are "The Covenant of the Baptist Alliance" and "An Address to the Public from the

Interim Steering Committee of the Cooperative Baptist Fellowship."
Two other documents, "Baptist Ideals" and "The People Called American Baptists" are included because they are such valuable but
overlooked documents. While the first comes from a group of Southern Baptist leaders and theologians in 1964 and the second comes
from a committee of the American Baptists in 1987, they contain
much that the global Baptist fellowship would embrace at the end
of the twentieth century. All of the eight documents have been
reproduced here in full. The only alterations I have made are where
inclusive language, apart from the Divine reference, could, and in my
judgment would, have been used if they had been written today.

Appendix I: "Towards A Baptist Identity"

Appendix II: "Baptist Distinctives and Diversities"

Appendix III: "A Pronouncement on Religious Liberty"

Appendix IV: "The Covenant of the Alliance of Baptists"

Appendix V: "The Baptist Doctrine of The Church"

Appendix VI: "An Address To The Public"

Appendix VII: "Baptist Ideals"

Appendix VIII: "The People Called American Baptists:
                   A Confessional Statement"

"TOWARDS A BAPTIST IDENTITY"

[This statement, in my judgment, is the single best statement of the Baptist identity issued by a group of Baptists in the twentieth century. It comes from the Commission on Baptist Heritage of the Baptist World Alliance and was ratified by the Commission in July, 1989. It deserves wide circulation as an excellent representation of Baptist beliefs and commitments. The document may also be found in William H. Brackney, editor, Faith, Life and Witness: The Papers of the Study and Research Division of The Baptist World Alliance, 1986–1990 *(Birmingham, AL: Samford University Press, 1986).]*

"TOWARDS A BAPTIST IDENTITY: A STATEMENT RATIFIED BY THE BAPTIST HERITAGE COMMISSION IN ZAGREB, YUGOSLAVIA JULY, 1989"

Preamble
This statement on Baptist identity was produced by the Commission on Baptist Heritage as a working document for the 1986–90 Quinquennium and arises out of a brain-storming exercise at their Singapore meeting. It is deliberately intended to be a *descriptive* rather than a *credal* statement, and it is recognized that there may well need to be flexibility in translation for use in particular local situations.

The Scriptures
Baptists start with the Scriptures, which afford us God's self-revelation, first in the unfolding of a concern for His People, but supremely in the life, death and resurrection of Jesus Christ. The Scriptures, as related by the Holy Spirit to our contemporary situation, are our authority in all matters of faith and practice.

What is the Gospel?

Men and women everywhere are alienated from God and from the world as God designed it. The Biblical word for this is Sin, which the Bible says is so serious that we cannot remedy this condition ourselves: there must be a radical new start which, in John 3, Jesus calls the "new birth." The first word of the Christian gospel must always be Grace: not what we aspire to do but what God has done for us without any claim or work on our part. The grace of God, expressed in the crucifixion of Jesus Christ, makes possible the restoration of the relationship with God that sin has spoiled. But this grace which is God's free gift to all of us, like every other gift, has to be received or accepted for its purpose to be secured. This is the response that the Scriptures call Faith: a free, total and unconditional entrusting of our lives to Almighty God. We are invited to put our trust in Jesus Christ because, in Him, God has reached out to touch our sinful humanity.

Clearly this is an action that no one can take for anyone else—each individual must make a free and unfettered response for him/herself. Equally clearly, that act of trust must involve an intention to obey God's declared will, for unless this be so, the word trust is evacuated of all possible meaning and effectiveness.

What is the Church?

Unlike many others, Baptists do not define the church in terms of structures of ministry or by the regular celebration of the ordinances. Rather, they believe that as individuals come to put their trust in God and confess Christ as Savior and Lord (which they believe to be the scriptural conditions for baptism), so the church is created. This is why they have been advocates of what has been called the Believers' Church or the Gathered Community (of believers gathered out of the world). From this conviction as to the nature of the church as constituted by believers covenanting together in common confession of the name of Jesus, it is seen that their practice of confining baptism (by immersion) to believers only, is entirely logical.

A local church so constituted represents in any place the church in that locality; it is fully the church, not a branch of some national or wider institution. Under the Lordship of Christ and before the open Scriptures, it is competent, when properly summoned, in church meeting to govern itself, to determine a strategy for mission in its locality, and to appoint its ministers (deacons and pastors) and other officers. These officers will serve its interests and execute its will in matters pastoral, educational and practical, but the first authority for all decision-making in a Baptist church must remain in whole church meeting.

Baptist churches reject all state interference in their activities. Each local church is free, and indeed duty-bound by the concerns of the gospel, to enter into covenant relationship with other Christians, both nationally and locally. In Baptist life, relationships have traditionally been in associations, conventions and unions, in support of missionary work at home and abroad, and internationally through the Baptist World Alliance.

Baptists ordain men, and in some, but not all parts of the family, women to the Ministry of the Word, and expect their ministries to be respected for their sacred calling. The witness and service of the church is not seen by Baptists, however, as exclusively the work of the ordained ministry but as inclusively the responsibility of the whole membership.

Most Baptists find no difficulty in a lay person celebrating at the Lord's Table or in the Baptismal Pool, ordinances which are seen by Baptists as symbolic of the death and resurrection of Jesus, and of each believer's identification, by faith, with Him, in both dying to sin and rising to new life in Him. This same Christocentric gospel is preached from Baptist pulpits Sunday by Sunday, for proclamation retains a central place in Baptist worship.

What is Discipleship?

Personal commitment is the starting point for every Christian, yet all need to discover the corporate dimension of the church: in common worship, in generous giving to fellowship needs, and in loyal participation in the mission of the local church.

Baptists are an evangelistic people who have always been committed to sharing their faith, to the extension of the church, and for the last two hundred years to overseas mission as well. In the name of their Lord they have given themselves to the care of the needy and oppressed. Increasingly in the twentieth century (although also in earlier times), they have seen the need to speak and act prophetically, denouncing structural evil wherever it puts God's "Shalom" at risk. Opposed to everything that denies the rule of Christ, some even suffer imprisonment and martyrdom for their steadfast witness, imposing an obligation on all the family to support them in both prayer and action.

Recognizing the vast demands of Christian witness and discipleship, Baptists have always been a praying people, in both corporate prayer and in encouraging a pattern of individual spirituality that requires each church member to engage in regular prayer and Bible study, for the whole of Scripture rather than abstracted creed is for Baptists the determinant alike of corporate belief and individual action.

Because Baptists delay baptism until an individual has made a personal confession of faith, they are especially concerned for the Christian nurture of children and young people until they come to acknowledge Christ as Savior for themselves, thus fulfilling promises made at services of thanksgiving and blessing that they have become a common celebration of the gift of children among Baptists.

Baptists were among the first to campaign for liberation of opinion and religious practice, not only for themselves but for all people, including the unbeliever, for they believed that each individual needed to be free to make choices about faith and commitment unfettered by any outside agency. Such freedom has led the Baptists to be a diverse people with no over-arching rule demanding common thought or practice among them. But amidst that diversity there is a unity because freedom from the state or from ecclesiastical hierarchies has also meant freedom to develop in each situation a style of churchmanship which, under the guidance of the Holy Spirit, they believe best serves the interests of the kingdom.

Many of the characteristics described here, if not all, are held by other Christian groups. Baptist distinctiveness is best seen in holding all these attitudes together in a way that is at once loyal to the traditions of Reformed Christianity without being sectarian. They are aware that they are but one part of the whole family of Christ's church here on earth, and seek in different ways (some within and others outside formal ecumenical structures) to lend support to the whole of the Church's work at the witness to the kingdom that Jesus proclaimed.

Baptists are:

—members of the whole Christian family who stress the experience of personal salvation through faith in Jesus, symbolized both in baptism and the Lord's Supper;
—those who under the Lordship of Jesus Christ have bonded together in free local congregations, together seeking to obey Christ in faith and in life;
—those who follow the authority of Scriptures in all matters of faith and practice;
—those who have claimed religious liberty for themselves and all people;
—those who believe that the Great Commission to take the Gospel to the whole world is the responsibility of the whole membership.

"BAPTIST DISTINCTIVES AND DIVERSITIES"

[Because the introductory paragraphs of this document explain its nature and origins, this statement of the Baptist identity needs no lengthy explanation. Two points need to be underscored, however. One, the importance of the statement is found in the fact that it represents not one but six different Baptist bodies within the United States. Two, the document is unique in describing "disagreements and differences" among Baptists, as well as identifying the common convictions of Baptists. This two-fold approach aids in sharpening the commonly accepted Baptist identity and precludes theological emphases that deviate from this broader norm. The document was published in pamphlet form by The Judson Press.]

"BAPTIST DISTINCTIVES AND DIVERSITIES AND DISAGREEMENTS AND DIFFERENCES OF EMPHASIS AMONG BAPTISTS"

1964
Baptist Jubilee Advance

The material in this paper is written in two parts. The first part deals with "Baptist Distinctives" and the second part with "Disagreements and Differences of Emphasis Among Baptists." It is not to be considered as an official document of any Baptist body, although it was written by a committee representative of six Baptist groups in North America as a "starting point" for discussion in local churches and at the 1964 Third Baptist Jubilee Celebration to be held in Atlantic City, New Jersey, May 22–24. It may be reprinted without permission in full, but it is hoped that no reproduction of parts of the text will be made unless the entire text is also reprinted. Already much material has been compressed by the committee into very small space, and further reduction will serve only to distort the intent of the authors.

The B.J.A. committee that authorized the writing of this material hopes that it can and will serve as a starting point for discussion in local churches in the spring of 1964 and will also be useful later that year and in several years to come. The papers will be presented officially to the Jubilee Advance meeting in Atlantic City in May and will be discussed in open forum there by three representatives of each cooperating Baptist body before the messengers that attend that gathering. Further clarification and discussion at that time, it is hoped, will serve to extend the discussion among the churches as they seek to continue the cooperation begun during the five year B.J.A. program.

Members of the committee that produced this document are:

Dr. R. F. Aldwinckle, Baptist Federation of Canada, chairman
Dr. Robert G. Torbet, American Baptist Convention
Dr. C. M. Smith, National Baptist Convention, Inc.
Dr. D. J. Draewell, North American Baptist General Conference
Dr. Melvin G. Nida, Seventh Day Baptist General Conference
Dr. E. S. James, Southern Baptist Convention

BAPTIST DISTINCTIVES

Introduction

Baptists, from their organized beginnings in the early seventeenth century, have tenaciously held dear certain basic convictions. Some of these they have borrowed from other Christians. Some were the results of their fresh understanding of the Word of God and the world of men. The validity of many of these insights has, through the years, brought about their adoption by other Christian groups as well.

It would not be true, therefore, to say that any one Baptist conviction is held today by Baptists only. It is true, however, that they hold them in combination in a manner not found in other churches.

This combination results in a Christian witness which is peculiarly and distinctively Baptist.

Authority

Christ as Lord of the Believer

The foundation truth upon which Baptists build is the Lordship of Christ over the individual believer. All other authorities are judged by the authority of the Son of God. Ultimate loyalty, therefore, is given to a Person, rather than to creeds, books, historic patterns, or effective procedures. Christ's will is mandatory for the believer. Joyful submission and purposeful obedience to the Savior form the essence of the Christian life.

Christ as Head of the Church

Just as Christ is confessed as Lord of the individual believer, so also Baptists recognize him as head of the church. He is head of the church in its expression within a local congregation. He is likewise head of the church in its wider expression which includes all those redeemed by his grace. No vicar, pope, bishop, prophet, elder, minister, priest, council, synod, or convention can usurp the primacy of Christ's authority. Neither may anything or anyone interfere with the directness of that authority to the church. The church, therefore, never moves with greater sureness, purpose, and victory than when it acknowledges its proper relationship to Jesus Christ. In the imagery of Scripture, we confess that the body must submit to the head.

The Scriptures

The Bible has always been recognized by Baptists as having a unique role and character. For them, the inspired Scriptures possess authority in all matters of faith and practice. Though not known as a creedal people, Baptists have, nevertheless, at times found it helpful to use creeds or confessions of faith. These have been used primarily as instruments to systematize and summarize certain biblical truths. Such formulated statements, however, have never been accorded the same status as Scripture. They have always been recognized as deriving their authority from the Bible; moreover, their validity had always been judged by the Scriptures.

Christian Experience

Spiritual Rebirth

Baptists understand the Bible to teach that it is by a personal spiritual rebirth that one becomes a member of the family of God. This regenerating experience can be effected within a human life only by the power of a gracious and loving God. No boasting or other expressions of personal pride are, therefore, appropriate to one who has been the recipient of such redemptive grace.

Human Response

Though salvation is of God, people must make the proper response to this divine provision for their need. Their response begins with an acknowledgement of sin and estrangement from God. It continues with sincere repentance. It includes also personal faith in the One who reconciles people to God.

The Church

The Universal Church

Many early Baptists in their confessional statements express a belief in the church universal as composed of all who truly profess faith in Jesus Christ as Lord and Saviour by whatever denominational name they are known. They also indicated their understanding of the church as being visibly expressed in local congregations where the gospel was truly preached, the ordinances rightly administered, and the discipline of holiness maintained. This dual understanding of the church has been maintained by Baptists to the present day and is a viewpoint which allows them to recognize other communions as fellow Christians.

A Fellowship of Believers

Baptists began with the conviction that the church is a fellowship of believers who, upon personal repentance and profession of faith, have been incorporated into the body of Christ through the activity of the

Holy Spirit. Thus they stand apart from those who assume that citizenship in a "Christian" nation, membership in a "Christian" family, living within the geographical boundaries of a church parish, or receiving baptism as an infant places one within the church. Personal Christian experience always precedes church membership. Within the fellowship of believers Baptists find nurture for their Christian experience to help then grow into the fullness of the stature of Christ.

Baptism by Immersion

The ordinance of baptism is the act of entry into fellowship of the local church. Their study of the New Testament led Baptists to conclude that only immersion has Scriptural authority as a mode of baptism. The meaning of the originally-used Greek words, the contexts of Scriptural descriptions of the act, and the historic evidence of early church practice support this contention. The symbolism of baptism revealed in Scripture, which portrays death, burial and resurrection, has confirmed Baptists in their conviction that only immersion speaks clearly of the meaning of this ordinance.

Baptists also baptize none but believers. Since baptism is an outward expression of an inward experience, the former has no meaning apart from the latter. Thus, baptism of infants who are incapable of personal faith, mass baptism of peoples without due regard for their personal relationship to God, and baptism of the unconscious or dead have not been practiced.

Baptism is not viewed by Baptists as mediating in any way the saving grace of God to the individual. It is seen rather as one of the significant first acts of obedience to be performed by the individual who has experienced spiritual rebirth. In the waters of baptism, one thus reveals symbolically death to an old life and resurrection by God's Spirit to a new life in Christ. This act is attended by God's blessing upon the one who so confesses faith and also upon the community of believers who witness this profession.

The Lord's Supper

The second ordinance administered by the church is that of the Lord's Supper. While Baptists reject doctrines of transubstantiation and consubstantiation, they, nevertheless, find genuine spiritual renewal through the observance of this memorial feast. The memory of Christ's sufferings and death brings to the believer the wholesome experiences of self-examination, repentance, a new-found sense of communion with God, a purposeful dedication to the divine will, and a new loyalty to the body of Christ.

Democratic Government

Since the church is composed of the redeemed who have equal access to the presence, mind, and will of God, Baptists are convinced that the local church should be governed democratically by its own congregation. While it is not assumed that church decisions democratically arrived at always reflect the will of God, it is assumed that a spiritually sensitive congregation is less likely to misinterpret the divine will than an individual believer. The New Testament gives prominence to the congregation and the local expression of the priesthood of believers.

An Ordained Ministry

An ordained clergy has always been a part of Baptist structure. Ordination is a formal recognition that God has given a set-apart ministry to the church, that he has called people into his service, endowed them with spiritual gifts to bless the church, and, further, that the candidates have taken seriously the divine call by giving evidence of thorough preparation and a holy life. Ordination is an act of the local church and is conferred following the recommendation of a council, composed of ordained and lay representatives of other churches, which examines the candidate.

Principle of Association

Baptist churches have recognized from the beginning of their history that loyalty to the New Testament requires them to associate together. The practical values of so doing have been recognized and appreciated by them. They have found in their conventions, conferences, federations and unions satisfying opportunities for fellowship, mutual encouragement, corporate witness, evangelization, missionary outreach, and other expressions of Christian concern. The relation of the local church to the larger organization, though recognized as important, has always been a voluntary one.

Freedom

Individual Liberty

Baptists have long pled for and have practiced consistently religious liberty for all. Today, although zealous to propagate their own convictions, they refuse to use physical, economic, or political intimidation to obtain converts. They also vigorously protest the use of these tactics by others.

Baptists further believe that every follower of Jesus Christ is free to come to God without the mediation of a priestly class which has an exclusive control over the dispensing of divine favor. The Christian is free to read the Bible and be guided to its meaning by the Holy Spirit. In becoming a part of the witness of a local church, however, his freedom in doctrinal interpretation and personal behavior is tempered by the convictions and needs of the community of believers.

Church Liberty

Baptists believe that a local church is free to make and carry out the policies and programs which best reflect and fulfill God's purpose for the church. The church always has the obligation to give heed to the direction of Jesus Christ, and must be free to do so. This freedom is conditioned by the fact that each church bears a living relationship to the total body of Christ. In the words of Scripture: "the eye cannot say unto the hand, I have no need of thee."

In Relation to the State

Closely related to the understanding of Baptists concerning individual and church freedom is their conviction that there must be a basic separation between church and state. It is recognized that God has given legitimate roles to church and state which both must carry out in the world of men and women. The state's primary responsibility is to people as citizens. The church's primary responsibility is to those who are its members. The state's primary functions are to exercise civil authority, maintain law and order, and promote public welfare. The church's primary functions are to witness to the gospel of Jesus Christ and to build up believers in their faith. Since the constituencies and functions of the church and the state respectively are not identical, each must maintain separate administrations, separate sources of support, and separate educational programs.

Mission

Proclamation of the Gospel

Baptists declare that the proclamation of the gospel is central to their task in the world. They recognize the gospel to be God's good news to humankind. This good news touches the whole person. It bears upon intellectual, emotional, physical and social needs. It offers forgiveness for past failures, strength for present testings, and hope for life's future experiences. Baptists realize that proclaiming the gospel involves more than speaking of its truths. It means allowing the Holy Spirit to work creatively through one's total personality so that the dynamic power of Jesus Christ impinges upon people in their need.

Missionary Outreach

Recognizing the relevancy of the gospel for all, Baptists have demonstrated a missionary passion that has carried them to the ends of the earth. The knowledge of human need and God's provision to meet it have offered sufficient motivation for missionaries to endure hardship and death in their efforts to serve as ambassadors of Jesus Christ. The daring faith of these women and men has so inspired Baptists, that they find it easier to rally to the support of this aspect of their Christian responsibility than to almost any other. Baptists believe that the gospel of Christ "is the power of God unto salvation to everyone that believeth."

DISAGREEMENTS AND DIFFERENCES OF EMPHASIS AMONG BAPTISTS

Introduction

In view of the historic Baptist emphasis upon soul-liberty and freedom of conscience, it is not surprising to find both in the past and today considerable diversity of theological and practical emphases among Baptists. This does not prevent our acknowledgement of certain convictions held in common and our desire to claim the descriptive name of Baptists. If, however, our unity as Baptists is to be deepened and mutual understanding increased, it is desirable that our differences should be honestly understood and charitably discussed. This is the underlying purpose of what follows.

Theological Differences

It is important to realize that these differences are not between Unions and Conventions but between individual Baptists. No single Baptist Convention can be readily characterized by one theological label, since the differences here to be mentioned are often found within the same Baptist body. It is true that Seventh Day Baptists have a name which underlines a special emphasis among them; yet they obviously share many other convictions which are common to all Baptists, they clearly regard themselves as members of the Baptist movement, and entertain theological differences within their fellowship. With these comments in mind, the chief theological differences may be listed as they affect the following topics:

The Inspiration and Authority of Scripture

While all Baptists acknowledge the inspiration and authority of Scripture, it is clear that there is great diversity among us in regard to principles of interpretation, the nature and manner of inspiration, the precise way in which Scripture is understood in the light of the final authority of Christ Himself. Problems of authorship and historicity, the nature of Biblical language and the meaning of terms such as "literal" and "symbolic," the legitimacy of a scholarly approach to the Scriptures and the limits of such a treatment of the Bible—all these

are matters on which no complete unanimity is to be found among
Baptists. This is not necessarily to be deplored provided such differences are anchored in a sincere loyalty to the Scriptures and to Jesus
Christ as Lord and Saviour. Nor can Baptists with their emphasis
upon freedom rightly expect complete uniformity in the language
used to express our deepest convictions about God and Christ.

Millennialism

While many Baptists hold some form of millennial doctrine, this is
by no means true of all, and such differences exist within the same
Conventions. This is a matter of differing individual interpretations
of Scripture which cut across the boundaries which separate one group
of Baptists from another.

Salvation for All or for Some Only

Differences of understanding concerning eternal punishment and the
possible salvation of all have marked Baptists throughout their history,
as well as contrasting views concerning the universal scope of the
Atonement or its limitation to the elect. Such problems are still with
us, and are becoming live issues in some quarters. It is imperative that
Baptists try sympathetically to understand each other, even when
complete theological agreement is difficult.

The Sabbath Day

The Seventh Day Baptists have their own special emphasis concerning
the continued observance of the Sabbath. Although this is not widely
shared by Baptists, it needs to be understood. Their emphasis also
underlines the necessity for a more thorough investigation by all Baptists as to the true meaning and significance of Sunday and its modern
observance.

Differences of Judgment Concerning
the Nature of the Church

Only a brief list can here be given without detailed explanation or
discussion, but the following points emerge when any representative
group of Baptists meet to discuss such matters.

The Autonomy of the Local Church

How far does our historic emphasis upon true autonomy of the local church do justice to such a New Testament expression as "the Body of Christ" interpreted in the wider and more comprehensive sense?

The Theological Status of Associations and Conventions

While all Baptists wish to retain the prerogatives of the local church in matters of self-government and control of its internal affairs, others are not happy to regard wider groupings of local churches, such as Associations, Unions and Conventions as having their justification only in expediency and practical necessities. Such co-operative action by local churches in a wider fellowship would be regarded by these Baptists as being a legitimate and further expression of the nature of the body of Christ. Indeed, a significant minority might want to speak of the Church in this wider manifestation in addition to its application to the local church. Some Baptists feel strongly that our fear of delegating authority and of indirect democracy is seriously impeding the more effective unity of action among Baptists for which, in their opinion, the present situation calls.

Baptism and Church Membership

Important differences appear in regard to Believers' Baptism and its relation to church membership. Some churches limit membership to immersed believers only (closed membership); others admit membership on profession of faith and leave the question of baptism to the conscience of the believer (open membership). In recent years a mediating position has been adopted where Christians from other denominations, not baptized as believers, are admitted to a more active membership but are not generally given the privileges of voting for the call of a minister or of acting as a delegate to associations or conventions. This practice, often described as associate membership, is found in some churches in both the United States and Canada.

In addition, there are many Baptists who refuse to regard as valid a baptism administered by other than what they consider a New Testament church (alien baptism). Others feel equally strongly that the presence of genuine faith and the reality of the new birth should be the only measurement of a true baptism, even when the baptism is performed in a non-Baptist church.

While it is fair to say that almost all Baptists today regard immersion as the New Testament mode of baptism, some hesitate to make the mode a theological absolute on the ground that the spiritual realities to which believers' baptism testifies are more important than the symbolic form.

Closely connected with this question is that of attendance at the Lord's Supper. Many closed membership churches practice dosed communion, i.e., they admit to the Lord's Supper only immersed believers. Others observe "open" communion, i.e., they invite all who accept Jesus as Lord and Saviour to participate, leaving it to the individual conscience to accept or refuse the invitation thus given.

Separation of Church and State

Baptists are unanimous in declaring that the state must not exercise direct control over the church, interfere with its free self-government under Christ, or bring legal pressure to bear upon the individual in matters of religious faith and practice. In practice, however, Baptists in different parts of the world interpret the application of this principle in varying ways. The crucial questions are as follows:

1. How far should Baptist churches and Baptist individuals accept tax concessions and other benefits from a State which is friendly to the Christian religion and desires to support it?

2. Does the separation of Church and State mean the complete elimination from State-controlled public schools of all forms of religious worship and instruction?

3. Can Baptists support the teaching of religion in State schools by ministers, whether Baptists or clergy of other denominations? (This has special relevance to the Canadian situation.)

4. How much and what kind of State financial aid can be offered to and received by church-related schools?

The Ecumenical Movement

This is perhaps one of the most serious of all recent differences of opinion among Baptists. Lack of knowledge and strong emotional reaction make difficult a patient and fair study of the problem, and call for immediate consideration. While Baptists have a form of ecumenicity in the Baptist World Alliance, some feel that this is not enough and that Baptists cannot refuse to consider their relationship to other Christian bodies. The main points at issue would appear to be the following:

1. Does closer co-operation with other Christian bodies mean the acceptance of local comity arrangements which would restrict our freedom to make the Baptist witness wherever the spirit of God leads us so to do?

2. Must membership of the World Council of Churches lead to the organic union of all existing churches with the consequent disappearance of Baptists as a separate denomination and the danger of an eventual super-Church that would be a threat to religious liberty? To this some Baptists would say "yes." Others would maintain that the constitution of the World Council of Churches safeguards the full freedom of the participating churches; they suggest that the precise nature of Christian unity has yet to be agreed upon, and that the danger of a super-Church is increased by the absence from such theological discussions of those who have been historically committed to religious liberty. The basic theological difference would seem to be between those who make the Baptist view of the church normative and those who believe that Baptists form one part of the universal church. This means a readiness on the part of Baptists to acknowledge that other denominations are also parts of the one universal church and that loyalty to Christ demands our willingness to seek a more adequate expression of the unity that is already ours in Christ.

3. Some Baptists have accepted the charge of "modernism" or "liberalism" levelled in some quarters against the World Council of Churches. Others reply that since every kind of church tradition and every shade of theological opinion is represented in the Council, the imposition of such a label is both unfair and untrue to the facts of

the case. Since there is much diversity of theological views even among Baptists themselves, the same condition is certainly to be expected in a body as large as the World Council of Churches. Baptists generally, whatever their differences in this matter, would agree that the World Council of Churches is not above criticism, that Christian unity is primarily a matter of the spirit and not of organization only, and that unity, however defined, must not be purchased at the expense of truth or by the sacrifice of convictions honestly and sincerely held.

The Christian Gospel
In Relation To Social Problems

Differences among individual Baptists can be classified as follows:

Social Justice
Some put the stress upon the responsibility to evangelize individuals only; others upon the application of Christian principles to political and economic life. Some would attempt to combine both, seeing evangelism as the total witness of Christians' lives in all of their relationships in society.

Race Problems
Some Baptists would be willing to concede complete equality of opportunity to all peoples regardless of color, nationality, or creed; some are not willing to do so.

War and Peace
Baptists from the seventeenth century onwards have always had in their ranks those who maintain a strictly pacifist position and refuse to bear arms for religious reasons. Others, while deploring war and admitting its evils, believe that under certain circumstances the Christian may be left with no alternative but to use force, even if this should mean nuclear weapons.

Worship and Evangelism

It should also be noted that there are significant differences of emphasis among Baptists in their manner of conducting public worship. Some would stress the freedom of the Spirit and the informal nature of worship; others believe that the reality of the Spirit's presence is not incompatible with a more formal and liturgical form of service. Some incline more to what has been called "mass evangelism," while others prefer the various forms of personal evangelism through Christian education and individual witness. Some churches regularly give a call to public decision as part of the act of worship; for others this is not a customary practice and is reserved for special occasions. These factors result in differences of spirit and atmosphere from one local church to another and even between geographical areas and countries. These matters are not occasions of serious difference among us. Nevertheless they may well be noted in this connection.

"A PRONOUNCEMENT ON RELIGIOUS LIBERTY"

[The following statement on religious liberty was adopted unanimously in 1939 by The National Baptist Convention (September 20, 1939), The Northern Baptist Convention (June 21, 1939), and The Southern Baptist Convention (May 20, 1939). As such the document is important because it represents the point of view of the three largest Baptist denominations in the United States at that time. While the document focuses on religious liberty, you will discover with a close reading that it identified other major Baptist distinctives. The copy printed below is copied from the 1939 Southern Baptist Convention Annual, *114–16.]*

"A PRONOUNCEMENT UPON RELIGIOUS LIBERTY"

No issue in modern life is more urgent or more complicated than the relation of organized religion to organized society. The sudden rise of the European dictators to power has changed fundamentally the organic law of the governments through which they exercise sovereignty, and as a result, the institutions of religion are either suppressed or made subservient to the ambitious national programs of these new totalitarian states.

Four Theories of the Relation of Church and State

There are four conceptions of the relation of church and state:

1. The Church is above the State, a theory held by those who claim that their ecclesiastical head is the vicar of Christ on earth.
2. The Church is alongside of the State, a theory held by the State Churches of various countries.

3. The State is above the Church, a theory held by the totalitarian governments.

4. The Church is separate from the State, championed by the Baptists everywhere, and held by those governments that have written religious liberty into their fundamental laws.

Baptists Opened the Door of Religious Liberty

Three hundred years have passed since the establishment under Baptist leadership of the first civil government in which full religious liberty was granted to the citizens forming the compact. The original document preserved in the City Hall, Providence, Rhode Island, is a covenant of citizens: "We, whose names are hereunder, desirous to inhabit in the town of Providence, do promise to subject ourselves in active or passive obedience to all such orders or agreements as shall be made for public good for the body in an orderly way, by the major assent of the present inhabitants, masters of families, incorporated together into a town fellowship, and such others whom they shall admit unto themselves only in civil things." These four concluding words opened wide the door to religious liberty.

Provide an Asylum for the Persecuted

This document was written three hundred years ago by Roger Williams, a Baptist minister and a student under Lord Coke, who had been banished from the Colony of Massachusetts for his espousal of the freedom of conscience. The founder of a civil commonwealth, called the Providence Plantations, he started a political movement which made the colony of Rhode Island the asylum of the persecuted and the home of the free.

Laid the Foundations of Religious Liberty

The Baptists of England, through Leonard Busher, had in 1614 pleaded with James I for freedom of conscience. Roger Williams became the apostle of religious liberty in colonial America. Dr. John Clarke, the pastor of the Baptist church of Newport, Rhode Island, as agent of the Rhode Island Colony and Providence Plantations, secured from Charles II in 1663 a charter in which the religious liberty claimed by the colonists was guaranteed through a royal decree. For the first time in the history of the world a civil government was founded that guaranteed to its inhabitants absolute religious freedom.

Pleaded for the Religious Rights of All

The Baptists of the Colony of Virginia, where between 1767 and 1778 forty-two Baptist ministers were jailed for preaching the gospel, through repeated memorials pleaded with the authorities for religious liberty. Favored by the leadership of Thomas Jefferson, James Madison, George Mason, John Leland and other lovers of freedom, they secured the free exercise of religion through the passage of the Bill of Rights in 1785. Not content with the winning of religious equality in Virginia, Baptists scrutinized the terms of the Federal Constitution and were largely instrumental in securing the passage of the First Amendment, which declares that "Congress shall make no law respecting an establishment of religion, or prohibiting the free exercise thereof." As to this, see the letter of George Washington to the Baptists of Virginia.

Religious liberty, as our Baptist ancestors defined it, was an emancipation from governmental and all other coercive restrictions, that thwarted the free exercise of religion, or their high purpose to achieve a Christlike character.

Baptists Stress Spirituality

The principles that animate the activities of the Baptists, principles which they hold to be clearly taught in the New Testament, are the worth of the individual; the necessity of the new birth; the preservation of Christian truth in Christian symbols; spirituality, or the free pursuit of Christian piety; the persuading of others through personal testimony, by the life of example, the preaching of the Gospel, and the creation of Christian institutions to the end that the unbelieving will be reconciled to God through a personal faith in Jesus Christ; the organization of groups of obedient believers into churches of Christ, democratic in the processes and theocratic in the principles of their government, and the continued uplifting of human society through the spirit of Christ and the ideals of his kingdom, having as its final objective the establishment of the eternal, unchanging purpose of Almighty God in the hearts of humans and the institutions of humankind.

Affirm the Competency of the Human Soul in Religion

The conception of the dignity of the individual, as held by Baptists, is grounded in the conviction that every soul possesses the capacity and the inalienable right to deal with God for one's self, and to deprive any soul of this right of direct access to God is to usurp the prerogatives of the individual and the function of God.

Free Churches Within a Free State

Standing as we do for the principle of voluntariness in religion, grounded upon the competency of the human soul, Baptists are essentially antagonistic to every form of religious coercion or persecution. We admit to our membership only those who give evidence that they are regenerated, but we recognize gladly that the grace of God is not limited to those who apply to us, but that our spiritual fellowship embraces all who have experienced the new birth and are walking in newness of life, by whatever name they may be called. We hold that the church of Christ, which in the Bible is called "the body of Christ," is not to be identified with any denomination or church that seeks to exercise ecclesiastical authority, but includes all the regenerated whoever and wherever they are, as these are led by the Holy Spirit. This church is a body without formal organization, and therefore cannot enter into contractual relations on any basis with the State. For this reason, Baptists believe in Free Churches within a Free State.

Today Baptists Feel Constrained to Declare Their Position

Since every session of the Congress considers legislation that raises the question as to the relation of the Federal Government to the institutions and agencies of religion, and since recently many tendencies have appeared that involve the freedom of religion and conscience, and furthermore, since there are some state constitutions that do not have embodied in them the Bill of Rights of the Federal Constitution, Southern Baptists feel constrained to declare their position and their convictions.

The Trend Toward Paternalism

Today the trend of government, even in democratic countries, lies in the direction of greater centralization. The philanthropic activities of the churches within the United States are being taken over by the Government. The defective, the indigent, and the dependent groups of our social order have long been supported from public funds. The greatest charity agent on earth today is our Federal Government. More and more the people are looking to the State to provide. As a nation we are becoming paternalistic. Efforts are now being made to place in the hands of the government the pensioning of those who are employed by the churches and the agencies that serve them, to grant to sectarian schools financial aid from tax-raised funds, and to support from public funds institutions that are established and managed by sectarian bodies.

Baptists Condemn the Union of Church and State

Southern Baptists hold that coercion of religious bodies through special taxes, the use of tax-raised funds for sectarian schools, and the appropriation of public money to institutions created to extend the power and influence of any religious body, violate the spirit of the First Amendment and result in the union of State and Church.

Oppose Special Favors Extended to Any Ecclesiastical Body

We oppose the establishing of diplomatic relations with any ecclesiastical body, the extension of special courtesies by our government to any ecclesiastical official as such, and the employment of any of the branches of our national defense in connection with religious services that are held to honor any ecclesiastical leader. All such violations of principle must be resisted in their beginnings.

Citizens of Two Commonwealths

We acknowledge ourselves to be citizens of two commonwealths, one earthly, the United States, the other heavenly, the Kingdom of God; and we claim the right to be good citizens of both. We recognize the sovereignty of the state and we give allegiance to the state, but we cannot give to the state the control of our consciences. We must obey God rather than humans.

The government resorts to coercion; we use persuasion. The government has authority over the acts of its citizens; we have to do with their motives. The business of the government is to make good laws; our business is to make good citizens, who continue to demand the enactment of better laws, embodying higher and still higher ethical standards. The end of governmental administration is equal justice under law. The end of our endeavor is the establishment of the will of God in the hearts and institutions of people. If one of us accepts an office in the government, that one recognizes it not only as a public trust, but also as a divine entrustment; for the powers that be are ordained of God. In a democracy like ours, it is possible to be a loyal American and a devoted Christian. This is true because religious liberty is an essential part of our fundamental law.

Defenders of Religious Liberty

Believing religious liberty to be not only an inalienable human right, but indispensable to human welfare, Baptists must exercise themselves to the utmost in the maintenance of absolute religious liberty for their Jewish neighbors, their Catholic neighbors, their Protestant neighbors, and for everybody else. Profoundly convinced that any deprivation of this right is a wrong to be challenged, Baptists condemn every form of compulsion in religion or restraint of the free consideration of the claims of religion.

We stand for a civil state, "with full liberty in religious concernments."

W. O. Carver	W. T. Conner
Rufus W. Weaver	J. Clyde Turner
J. B. Lawrence	Theo. F. Adams
W. W. Hamilton	

"THE COVENANT OF THE ALLIANCE OF BAPTISTS"

[One of the first organizational responses of Moderates to the takeover of the Southern Baptist Convention by Fundamentalists was the organization of The Southern Baptist Alliance. The formation of the Alliance (its commonly accepted name) was announced on February 12, 1987. In 1992 it changed its name to The Alliance of Baptists, altering also the introductory paragraph to its covenant. When originally adopted, the introductory paragraph read as follows: "The Southern Baptist Alliance is an alliance of individuals and churches dedicated to the preservation of historic Baptist principles, freedoms and traditions and the continuance of our ministry and mission within the Southern Baptist Convention. As an alliance we commit ourselves to the following." Although clearly reflecting a number of the issues that were prominent in the Fundamentalist-Moderate Controversy of the Southern Baptist Convention in the 1980s, this is surely one of the best brief summaries of the Baptist profile in the twentieth century.]

"THE COVENANT OF THE ALLIANCE OF BAPTISTS"

In a time when historic Baptist principles, freedoms, and traditions need a clear voice, and in our personal and corporate response to the call of God in Jesus Christ to be disciples and servants in the world, we commit ourselves to:

—First, the freedom of the individual, led by God's Spirit within the family of faith, to read and interpret the Scriptures, relying on the historical understanding by the church and on the best methods of modern biblical study;

—Second, the freedom of the local church under the authority of Jesus Christ to shape its own life and mission, call its own leadership, and ordain whom it perceives as gifted for ministry, male or female;

—Third, the larger body of Jesus Christ, expressed in various Christian traditions, and to the cooperation with believers everywhere in giving full expression to the Gospel;

—Fourth, the servant role of leadership within the church, following the model of our Servant Lord, and to full partnership of all of God's people in mission and ministry;

—Fifth, theological education in congregations, colleges and seminaries characterized by reverence for biblical authority and respect for open inquiry and responsible scholarship;

—Sixth, the proclamation of the Good News of Jesus Christ and the calling of God to all peoples to repentance and faith, reconciliation and hope, social and economic justice;

—Seventh, the principle of a free church in a free state and to the opposition to any effect either by church or state to use the other for its own purposes.

"THE BAPTIST DOCTRINE OF THE CHURCH"

[The following statement was approved by the Council of the Baptist Union of Great Britain and Ireland in March, 1948. An extraordinarily lucid document, it is an effort on the part of Baptists of England and Ireland to describe their view of the church in the mid-twentieth century. Baptists of England have contributed to the wider Baptist movement far out of proportion to their present relatively small numbers. Any effort to understand the identity of Baptists should take seriously any pronouncement from that country.

Some Baptists in the United States, especially those influenced by Landmarkism and Fundamentalism, will find some rather unfamiliar notes being struck in this document. First, the recurring theme of freedom and liberty are found throughout the document. Second, a firm ecumenical note is sounded while Baptist distinctives are maintained. In fact, the first article in the document is that of "The One Holy Catholic Church." Third, worship, while guided by "spontaneity and freedom," is to be characterized by "disciplined preparation of every part of the service." Fourth, the ministry, although an exalted office, is a ministry of "a church and not only a ministry of an individual." All ministerial authority comes from Christ and "through the believing community." Fifth, Believers' Baptism and the Lord's Supper are portrayed as "sacraments" which are "means of grace."

The source for this document is Ernest A. Payne, The Baptist Union: A Short History *(London: The Carey Kingsgate Press Limited, 1958), pages 283–91. In the original document the notes were at the bottom of the pages. I have inserted these in the text to comport with the documentation for the rest of this book.]*

"The Baptist Doctrine Of The Church"

1. The Baptist Union of Great Britain and Ireland represents more than three thousand churches and about three hundred thousand members. Through its membership in the Baptist World Alliance it is in fellowship with other Baptist communities through the world numbering about thirteen million, who have accepted the responsibilities of full communicant membership.

Baptists have a continuous history in Great Britain since the beginning of the seventeenth century. Many of their principles, however, were explicitly proclaimed in the second half of the sixteenth century by the radical wing of the Reformation movement. They claim as their heritage also the great central stream of Christian doctrine and piety through the centuries, and have continuity with the New Testament Church in that they rejoice to believe and seek faithfully to proclaim the Apostolic Gospel and endeavour to build up the life of their churches after what seems to them the New Testament pattern.

The One Holy Catholic Church

2. Although Baptists have for so long held a position separate from that of other communions, they have always claimed to be part of the one holy catholic Church of our Lord Jesus Christ. They believe in the catholic Church as the holy society of believers in our Lord Jesus Christ, which He founded, of which He is the only Head, and in which He dwells by His Spirit, so that though manifested in many communions, organized in various modes, and scattered throughout the world, it is yet one in Him (See "The Baptist Reply to the Lambeth Appeal"). The Church is the Body of Christ and a chosen instrument of the divine purpose in history.

In the worship, fellowship and witness of the one Church we know ourselves to be united in the communion of saints, not only with all believers upon earth, but also with those who have entered into life everlasting.

The origin of the Church is in the Gospel—in the mighty acts of God, the Incarnation, Ministry, Death, Resurrection and Ascension of our Lord and the Descent of the Holy Spirit. Thus it is the power of God in Christ which created the Church and which sustains it through the centuries. It is historically significant that Christ, at the outset of His ministry, "chose twelve to be with Him" and gathered His people into a new community. In our judgment there is no evidence in the New Testament to show that He formally organized the Church, but He did create it. This "New Israel," the expansion of which is recorded in the Acts of the Apostles and the Epistles, is the heir to the "Old Israel," yet it is marked by vital and significant differences. It is based upon the New Covenant; membership is not constituted by racial origins but by a personal allegiance; the ritual of temple and synagogue has given place to the ordinances of the Gospel and the national consciousness has widened to world horizons.

The Messianic community was reborn by the events of the Gospel and is "a new creation." Therefore, whilst there is an historical continuity with the Old Israel, Old Testament analogies do not determine the character and structure of the New Testament Church.

The Structure of Local Baptist Churches

3. (a) It is in membership of a local church in one place that the fellowship of the one holy catholic Church becomes significant. Indeed, such gathered companies of believers are the local manifestation of the one Church of God on earth and in heaven. Thus the church at Ephesus is described, in words which strictly belong to the whole catholic Church, as "the church of God, which He hath purchased with His own blood" (Acts xx.28). The vital relationship to Christ which is implied in full communicant membership in a local church carries with it membership in the Church which is both in time and in eternity, both militant and triumphant. To worship and serve in such a local Christian community is, for Baptists, of the essence of Churchmanship.

Such churches are gathered by the will of Christ and live by the indwelling of His Spirit. They do not have their origin, primarily, in human resolution. Thus the Baptist Confession of 1677 (McGlothlin, 265) which deals at length with doctrine and church order, uses phrases which indicate that local churches are formed by the response of believers to the Lord's command. Out of many such phrases we may quote the following: "Therefore they do willingly consent to walk together according to the appointment of Christ." Churches are gathered "according to His mind, declared in His word." Membership was not regarded as a private option, for the CONFESSION continues: "All believers are bound to join themselves to particular churches when and where they have opportunity so to do." In our tradition discipleship involves both church membership and a full acceptance of the idea of churchmanship.

(b) The basis of our membership in the church is a conscious and deliberate acceptance of Christ as Saviour and Lord by each individual. There is, we hold, a personal crisis in the soul's life when a person stands alone in God's presence, responds to God's gracious activity, accepts His forgiveness and commits to the Christian way of life. Such a crisis may be swift and emotional or slow-developing and undramatic, and is normally experienced within and because of our life in the Christian community, but it is always a personal experience wherein God offers His salvation in Christ, and the individual, responding by faith, receives the assurance of the Spirit that by grace he or she is the child of God. It is this vital evangelical experience which underlies the Baptist conception of the Church and is both expressed and safeguarded by the sacrament of Believers' Baptism.

(c) The life of a gathered Baptist church centres in worship, in the preaching of the Word, in the observance of the two sacraments of Believers' Baptism and the Lord's Supper, in growth in fellowship and in witness and service to the world outside. Our forms of worship are in the Reformed tradition and are not generally regulated by liturgical forms. Our tradition is one of spontaneity and freedom, but we hold that there should be disciplined preparation of every part of the service. The sermon, as an exposition of the Word of God and a means of building up the faith and life of the congregation, has a central place in public worship. The scriptures are held by us to be the primary authority both for the individual in his or her belief and way of life and for the Church in its teaching and modes of government. It is the objective revelation given in scripture which is the safeguard against a purely subjective authority in religion. We firmly hold that each must search the scriptures for himself or herself and seek the illumination of the Holy Spirit to interpret them. We know also that Church history and Christian experience through the centuries are a guide to the meaning of scripture. Above all, we hold that the eternal Gospel—the life, death and resurrection of our Lord—is the fixed point from which our interpretation, both of the Old and New Testaments, and of later developments in the Church, must proceed.

The worship, preaching, sacramental observances, fellowship and witness are all congregational acts of the whole church in which each member shares responsibility, for all are held to be of equal standing in Christ, though there is a diversity of gifts and a difference of functions. This responsibility and this equality are focused in the church meeting which, under Christ, cares for the well-being of the believing community and appoints its officers. It is the responsibility of each member, according to one's gifts, to build up the life of sisters and brothers and to maintain the spiritual health of the church (Rom xv.14). It is the church meeting which takes the responsibility of exercising that discipline whereby the church withdraws from members who are unruly and have ceased to share in its convictions and life.

The church meeting, though outwardly a democratic way of ordering the affairs of the church, has deeper significance. It is the occasion when, as individuals and as a community, we submit ourselves to the guidance of the Holy Spirit and stand under the judgments of God that we may know what is the mind of Christ. We believe that the structure of local churches just described springs from the Gospel and best preserves its essential features.

(d) The Christian doctrine of the Trinity asserts a relationship of Persons within the Godhead, and God has revealed Himself in the Person of His Son, our Saviour Jesus Christ. Thus the Gospel is the basis of the Christian evaluation of men and women as persons. Behind the idea of the gathered church lies the profound conviction of the importance of each Christian's growth to spiritual maturity and of the responsibility which, as a member of the divine family, she or he should constantly exercise.

(e) Although each local church is held to be competent, under Christ, to rule its own life, Baptists, throughout their history, have been aware of the perils of isolation and have sought safeguards against exaggerated individualism. From the seventeenth century there have been "Associations" of Baptist churches which sometimes appointed Messengers; more recently, their fellowship with one another has been greatly strengthened by the Baptist Union, the Baptist Missionary Society and the Baptist World Alliance. In recent years, General Superintendents have been appointed by the Baptist Union to have the care of churches in different areas. Indeed, we believe that a local church lacks one of the marks of a truly Christian community if it does not seek the fellowship of other Baptist churches, does not seek a true relationship with Christians and churches of other communions and is not conscious of its place in the one catholic Church. To quote again from the Confession of 1677: "As each church and all the members of it are bound to pray continually for the good and prosperity of all the churches of Christ in all places; and upon occasions to further it . . . so the churches . . . ought to hold communion amongst themselves for their peace, increase of love and mutual edification."

The Ministry

(4) A properly ordered Baptist church will have its duly appointed officers. These will include the minister (or pastor), elders, deacons, Sunday school teachers and other church workers. The Baptist conception of the ministry is governed by the principle that it is a ministry of a church and not only a ministry of an individual. It is the church which preaches the Word and celebrates the sacraments, and it is the church which, through pastoral oversight, feeds the flock and ministers to the world. It normally does these things through the person of its minister, but not solely through the minister. Any member of the church may be authorized by it, on occasion, to exercise the functions of the ministry, in accordance with the principle of the priesthood of all believers, to preach the Word, to administer baptism, to preside at the Lord's table, to visit, and comfort or rebuke members of the fellowship.

Baptists, however, have had from the beginning an exalted conception of the office of the Christian minister and have taken care to call their pastors. The minister's authority to exercise the ministerial office comes from the call of God in personal experience, but this call is tested and approved by the church of which the minister is a member and (as is increasingly the rule) by the representatives of a large group of churches. Ministers receive intellectual and spiritual training and are then invited to exercise their gifts in a particular sphere. Ministerial authority, therefore, is from Christ through the believing community. It is not derived from a chain of bishops held to be lineally descended from the Apostles, and we gratefully affirm that to our non-episcopal communities, as to those episcopally governed, the gifts of the Spirit and the power of God are freely given.

Many among us hold that since the ministry is the gift of God to the Church and the call to exercise the functions of a minister comes from Him, a person who is so called is not only the minister of a local Baptist church but also a minister of the whole Church of Jesus Christ.

Ordination takes place when a person has satisfactorily completed college training and has been called to the pastorate of a local church, appointed to chaplaincy service or accepted for service abroad by the Committee of the Baptist Missionary Society. The ordination service is presided over by either the Principal of the college, a General Superintendent or a senior minister and is shared in by other ministers and lay representatives of the church. Though there is no prescribed or set form of service, it invariably includes either a personal statement of faith or answers to a series of questions regarding the faith. From the seventeenth century onwards, ordination took place with the laying on of hands: in the nineteenth century this custom fell into disuse, but is now again increasingly practiced.

The Sacraments

5. In the preceding sections we have sought to describe the life and ministry of Baptist churches. It is in their total activity of worship and

prayer, sacrament and service that the grace of God is continuously given to believing men and women.

We recognize the two sacraments of Believers' Baptism and the Lord's Supper as being of the Lord's ordaining. We hold that both are "means of grace" to those who receive them in faith, and that Christ is really and truly present, not in the material elements, but in the heart and mind and soul of the believer and in the Christian community which observes the sacrament. Our confidence in this rests upon the promises of Christ and not upon any power bestowed on the celebrant in virtue of ordination or succession in ministry. We believe it is important not to isolate the sacraments from the context of the total activity of the worshipping, believing and serving fellowship of the church.

Following the guidance of the New Testament we administer Baptism only to those who have made a responsible and credible profession of "repentance towards God and faith in the Lord Jesus Christ." Such persons are then immersed in the name of the Father, the Son and the Holy Spirit. Salvation is the work of God in Christ, which becomes operative when it is accepted in faith. Thus we do not baptize infants. There is, however, a practice in our churches of presenting young children at a service of public worship where the responsibilities of the parents and the church are recognized and prayers are offered for the parents and the child. Baptists believe that from birth all children are within the love and care of the heavenly Father and therefore within the operation of the saving grace of Christ; hence they have never been troubled by the distinction between baptized and unbaptized children. They have had a notable share with other groups of Christian people in service to children in Sunday schools, orphanages, education and child welfare.

We would claim that the baptism of believers by immersion is in accordance with and sets forth the central facts of the Gospel. It is an "acted creed." We value the symbolism of immersion following the Pauline teaching of the believer's participation in the death, burial and resurrection of our Lord (Rom vi.3). As a matter of history, however, the recovery of the truth that baptism is only for believers preceded by some years the return by Baptists to the primitive mode of baptizing by immersion, and it is a credible and responsible profession of faith on the part of the candidate for baptism which we hold to be essential to the rite. As a means of grace to the believer and to the church and as an act of obedience to our Lord's command, we treasure this sacrament. The New Testament clearly indicates a connection of the gift of the Holy Spirit with the experience of baptism which, without making the rite the necessary or inevitable channel of that gift, yet makes it the appropriate occasion of a new and deeper reception of it.

The Lord's Supper is celebrated regularly in our churches. The form of service, which is "congregational" and in which laypeople have a part, preserves the New Testament conception of the Supper as an act of fellowship, a community meal. Yet as baptism is more than a dramatic representation of the facts of our redemption, so the Communion Service is more than a commemoration of the last Supper and a showing forth "of the Lord's death until He come." Here the grace of God is offered and is received in faith; here the real presence of Christ is manifest in the joy and peace both of the believing soul and of the community; here we are in communion, not only with members in our church, not only with the Church militant on earth and triumphant in heaven, but also with our risen and glorified Lord.

Membership of our local churches is normally consequent on Believers' Baptism, but differences of outlook and practice exist amongst us. "Close Membership" Baptist churches receive into their membership only those who have professed their faith in Christ by passing through the waters of baptism: "Open Membership" churches, though they consist, in the main, of baptized believers, receive also those Christians who profess such faith otherwise than in Believers' Baptism.

Similar differences are to be found amongst us on the question of those who may partake of the Lord's Supper. "Close Communion" churches invite to the Lord's table only those baptized on profession of faith. "Open Communion" churches welcome to the service all "who love the Lord Jesus Christ in sincerity." These differences do not prevent churches of different types from being in communion one with another nor from co-operating in the work of the Baptist Union, the Baptist Missionary Society and the Baptist World Alliance. They are united in the conviction that, in New Testament teaching, personal faith in Christ is essential to the sacraments of the Gospel and the membership of the Church.

Church and State

6. Our conviction of Christ's Lordship over His church leads us to insist that churches formed by His will must be free from all other rule in matters relating to their spiritual life. Any form of control by the State in these matters appears to us to challenge the "Crown Rights of the Redeemer." We also hold that this freedom in Christ implies the right of the church to exercise responsible self-government. This has been the Baptist position since the seventeenth century, and it appears to us that the growth of the omnicompetent state and the threat to liberty which has appeared in many parts of the world today make more than ever necessary this witness to spiritual freedom and responsibility which has always been characteristic of the Baptist movement.

This freedom, however, has not led to irresponsibility in our duties as citizens. We believe it is a Christian obligation to honour and serve the State and to labour for the well-being of all men and women. Baptists have shared in many working-class movements, have a not undistinguished record in social service, and were pioneers in the modern missionary movement. They hold that there is a responsibility laid upon each member of the church and upon the churches themselves to apply their faith to all the perplexities of contemporary life.

It will be seen that in this statement of the doctrine of the Church the emphasis falls time and again upon the central fact of evangelical experience, that when God offers His forgiveness, love and power the gift must be personally accepted in faith by each individual. From this follows the believer's endeavour to walk in the way of the Lord and to be obedient to His commandments. From this follows, also, our traditional defence of civil and religious liberty. It governs our conception of the Church and our teaching on Believers' Baptism.

Gratefully recognizing the gifts bestowed by God upon other communions, we offer these insights which He has entrusted to us for the service of His whole Church.

BIBLIOGRAPHY

The Baptist Position. A Statement Prepared by the Commission on Baptist Principles and Policy for Study and Discussion within the Baptist Convention of Ontario and Quebec, 1947.

The Baptist Reply to the Lambeth Appeal, adopted by the Baptist Union Assembly, 4th May 1926 (reprinted by G. K. A. Bell, *Documents on Christian Union,* second series, 102ff.).

Carver, W. O., "Baptist Churches" in *The Nature of the Church.* A Report of the American Theological Committee (1945), of the Continuation Committee, World Conference on Faith and Order.Cook, Henry, *What Baptist Stand For.* Kingsgate Press, 1947.

Dakin, Arthur, *The Baptist View of the Church and Ministry,* Kingsgate Press, 1944.

Evans, P. W., *Sacraments in the New Testament.* Tyndale Press, 1947.

McGlothlin, W. J., *Baptist Confessions of Faith,* Baptist Historical Soc., 1911.

Payne, E. A., *The Baptist Movement in the Reformation and Onwards.* Kingsgate Press, 1947.

Payne, E. A., *The Fellowship of Believers: Baptist Thought and Practice Yesterday and Today,* Kingsgate Press, 1944. (Reprints part of the 1677 Confession of the Particular Baptists and the Reply to the Lambeth Appeal.)

Report of a Special Committee set up by the Baptist Union on the question of Union between Baptists, Congregationalists and Presbyterians, 1937.

Robinson, H. Wheeler, *Baptist Principles.* Kingsgate Press, third edition, 1938.

Robinson, H. Wheeler, *The Life and Faith of the Baptists.* revised edition, Kingsgate Press, 1946.

Underwood, A. C, *A History of English Baptists.* Kingsgate Press, 1947.

Walton, Robert C., *The Gathered Community.* Carey Press, 1946.

Whitley, W. T., *History of British Baptists.* Kingsgate Press, second edition, 1932.

"AN ADDRESS TO THE PUBLIC"

[The Cooperative Baptist Fellowship is a group of Moderate Southern Baptists and ex-Southern Baptists. Born in August, 1990, as a result of the Fundamentalist-Moderate Controversy within the Southern Baptist Convention (1979–1990), it did not adopt the name "Cooperative Baptist Fellowship" until May 10, 1991, and after the adoption of the following document. Because the name of the organization originally proposed was the "United Baptist Fellowship," that was the term used in this document when presented to the Assembly. It has been replaced here by "Cooperative Baptist Fellowship," the name ultimately adopted for the organization.

Presented to the General Assembly as "information" on behalf of the "Interim Steering Committee," the document is the result of the work of two people, Cecil E. Sherman and Walter B. Shurden. Sherman's is the primary hand. A brief history of the document is found in the archives of the Cooperative Baptist Fellowship at Mercer University in Macon, Georgia.

Designed primarily to distinguish Moderate Southern Baptists from Fundamentalist Southern Baptists, "An Address to the Public" gives insight into what Moderate Southern Baptists believe to be consistent with the Baptist tradition of freedom and responsibility. After providing a cursory background to the Fundamentalist-Moderate Controversy, the document lists some of the major issues in the conflict. It then commits Moderates to the building of a new organization that will embody Baptist principles and extend the missionary work of their people.]

"AN ADDRESS TO THE PUBLIC" FROM THE INTERIM STEERING COMMITTEE OF THE COOPERATIVE BAPTIST FELLOWSHIP ADOPTED ON MAY 9, 1991

Introduction

Forming something as fragile as the Cooperative Baptist Fellowship is not a move *we* make lightly. We are obligated to give some explanation for why *we* are doing what *we* are doing. Our children will know what *we* have done; they may not know why *we* have done what we have done. We have reasons for our actions. They are:

I. Our Reasons Are Larger Than Losing.

For twelve years the Southern Baptist Convention in annual session has voted to sustain the people who lead the fundamentalist wing of the SBC. For twelve years the SBC in annual session has endorsed the arguments and the rationale of the fundamentalists. What has happened is not a quirk or a flash or an accident. It has been done again and again.

If inclined, one could conclude that the losers have tired of losing. But the formation of the Cooperative Baptist Fellowship does not spring from petty rivalry. If the old moderate wing of the SBC were represented in making policy and were treated as welcomed representatives of competing ideas in the Baptist mission task, then we would co-exist, as we did for years, alongside fundamentalism and continue to argue our ideas before Southern Baptists.

But this is not the way things are. When fundamentalists won in 1979, they immediately began a policy of exclusion. Non-fundamentalists are not appointed to any denominational positions. Rarely are gentle fundamentalists appointed. Usually only doctrinaire fundamentalists, hostile to the purposes of the very institutions they control, are rewarded for service by appointment. Thus, the boards of SBC agencies are filled by only one kind of Baptist. And this is true whether the vote to elect was 60–40 or 52–48. It has been since 1979 a "winner take all." We have no voice.

In another day Pilgrims and Quakers and Baptists came to America for the same reason. As a minority, they had no way to get a hearing. They found a place where they would not be second-class citizens. All who attended the annual meeting of the SBC in New Orleans in June of 1990 will have an enlarged understanding of why our ancestors left their homes and dear ones and all that was familiar. So forming the Cooperative Baptist Fellowship is not something we do lightly. Being Baptist should ensure that no one is ever excluded who confesses, "Jesus is Lord" (Philippians 2:11).

II. Our Understandings Are Different.

Occasionally, someone accuses Baptists of being merely a contentious, controversial people. That may be. But the ideas that divide Baptists in the present "controversy" are the same ideas that have divided Presbyterians, Lutherans, and Episcopalians. These ideas are strong and central; these ideas will not be papered over. Here are some of these basic ideas:

1. *Bible.* Many of our differences come from a different understanding and interpretation of Holy Scripture. But the difference is not at the point of the inspiration or authority of the Bible. We interpret the Bible differently, as will be seen below in our treatment of the biblical understanding of women and pastors. We also, however, have a different understanding of the nature of the Bible. We want to be biblical—especially in our view of the Bible. That means that we dare not claim less for the Bible than the Bible claims for itself. The Bible neither claims nor reveals inerrancy as a Christian teaching. Bible claims must be based on the Bible, not on human interpretations of the Bible.

2. *Education.* What should happen in colleges and seminaries is a major bone of contention between fundamentalists and moderates.

Fundamentalists educate by indoctrination. They have the truth and all the truth. As they see it, their job is to pass along the truth they have. They must not change it. They are certain that their understandings of the truth are correct, complete and to be adopted by others.

Moderates, too, are concerned with truth, but we do not claim a monopoly. We seek to enlarge and build upon such truth as we have. The task of education is to take the past and review it, even criticize it. We work to give our children a larger understanding of spiritual and physical reality. We know we will always live in faith; our understandings will not be complete until we get to heaven and are loosed from the limitations of our mortality and sin.

3. Mission. What ought to be the task of the missionary is another difference between us. We think the mission task is to reach people for faith in Jesus Christ by preaching, teaching, healing and other ministries of mercy and justice. We believe this to be the model of Jesus in Galilee. That is the way he went about his mission task. Fundamentalists make the mission assignment narrower than Jesus did. They allow their emphasis on direct evangelism to undercut other biblical ministries of mercy and justice. This narrowed definition of what a missionary ought to be and do is a contention between us.

4. Pastor. What is the task of the pastor? They argue the pastor should be the ruler of a congregation. This smacks of the bishops's task in the Middle Ages. It also sounds much like the kind of church leadership Baptists revolted against in the seventeenth century.

Our understanding of the role of the pastor is to be a servant/ shepherd. Respecting lay leadership is our assignment. Allowing the congregation to make real decisions is of the very nature of Baptist congregationalism. And using corporate business models to "get results" is building the Church by the rules of a secular world rather than witnessing to the secular world by way of a servant Church.

5. Women. The New Testament gives two signals about the role of women. A literal interpretation of Paul can build a case for making women submissive to men in the Church. But another body of scripture points toward another place for women. In Gal. 3:27-28 Paul wrote, "As many of you as are baptized into Christ have clothed yourselves with Christ. There is no longer Jew or Greek, there is not longer slave or free, there is no longer male and female; for all of you are one in Christ Jesus" (NSRV).

We take Galatians as a clue to the way the Church should be ordered. We interpret the reference to women the same way we interpret the reference to slaves. If we have submissive roles for women, we must also have a place for the slaves in the Church.

In Galatians Paul follows the spirit of Jesus who courageously challenged the conventional wisdom of his day. It was a wisdom with rigid boundaries between men and women in religion and in public life. Jesus deliberately broke those barriers. He called women to follow him; he treated women as equally capable of dealing with sacred issues. Our model for the role of women in matters of faith is the Lord Jesus.

6. *Church.* An ecumenical and inclusive attitude is basic to our fellowship. The great ideas of theology are the common property of all the Church. Baptists are only a part of that great and inclusive Church. So, we are eager to have fellowship with our brothers and sisters in the faith and to recognize their work for our Savior. We do not try to make them conform to us; we try to include them in our design for mission. Mending the torn fabric of both Baptist and Christian fellowship is important to us. God willing, we will bind together the broken parts into a new company in preview of the great fellowship we shall have with each other in heaven.

It should be apparent that the points of difference are critical. They are the stuff around which a fellowship such as the Southern Baptist Convention is made. We are different. It is regrettable, but we are different. And perhaps we are most different at the point of spirit. At no place have we been able to negotiate about these differences. Were our fundamentalist brethren to negotiate, they would compromise. And that would be a sin by their understandings. So, we can either come to their position, or we can form a new fellowship.

III. We Are Called to Do More than Politic.

Some people would have us continue as we have over the last twelve years, and continue to work within the SBC with a point of view to change the SBC. On the face of it this argument sounds reasonable. Acting it out is more difficult.

To change the SBC requires a majority vote. To effect a majority in annual session requires massive, expensive, contentious activity. We have done this, and we have done it repeatedly.

But we have never enjoyed doing it. Something is wrong with a religious body that spends such energy in overt political activity. Our time is unwisely invested in beating people or trying to beat people. We have to define the other side as bad and we are good. There is division. The existence of the Cooperative Baptist Fellowship is a simple confession of that division; it is not the cause of that division.

We can no longer devote our major energies to SBC politics. We would rejoice, however, to see the SBC return to its historic Baptist convictions. Our primary call is to be true to our understanding of the gospel. We are to advance the gospel in our time. When we get to heaven, God is not going to ask us, "Did you win in Atlanta in June of 1991?" If we understand the orders we are under, we will be asked larger questions. And to spend our time trying to reclaim a human institution (people made the SBC; it is not a scriptural entity) is to make more of that institution than we ought to make. A denomination is a missions delivery system; it is not meant to be an idol. When we make more of the SBC than we ought, we risk falling into idolatry. Twelve years is too long to engage in political activity. We are called to higher purposes.

Conclusion

• That we may have a voice in our Baptist mission . . . for that is our Baptist birthright. . . .

• That we may work by ideas consistent with our understanding of the gospel rather than fund ideas than are not our gospel. . . .

• That we may give our energies to the advancement of the Kingdom of God rather than in divisive, destructive politics . . . .

For these reasons we form the Cooperative Baptist Fellowship. This does not require that we sever ties with the old Southern Baptist Convention. It does give us another mission delivery system, one more like our understanding of what it means to be Baptist and what it means to do gospel. Therefore, we create a new instrument to further the Kingdom and enlarge the Body of Christ.

"BAPTIST IDEALS"

[This statement was prepared for the 1964 celebration of the one hundred and fiftieth anniversary of the organization of the first Baptist national organization in America. Prepared by a committee chaired by Ralph A. Herring, pastor of the First Baptist Church of Winston-Salem, North Carolina, and eighteen Southern Baptist Convention leaders and scholars, it describes the Baptist concepts of religious authority, the individual, the Christian life, and the church. It also has a final section entitled "Our Continuing Task." Beneath each sub-section is a helpful summary sentence.]

I. AUTHORITY

1. Christ as Lord
The ultimate source of Christian authority is Jesus Christ the Lord. His lordship springs from his eternal deity and power—as the anointed Son of the sovereign God—and from his vicarious redemption and victorious resurrection. His authority is the expression of righteous love, infinite wisdom, and divine holiness. This authority applies to the totality of life. It supplies integrity and unity to Christian purpose, strength to Christian commitment, and motivation for Christian loyalty. It demands willing obedience to Christ's commandments, dedication to his service, fidelity to his kingdom, and the utmost devotion to him as living Lord.

The ultimate source of authority is Jesus Christ the Lord, and every area of life is to be subject to his Lordship.

2. The Scriptures
The Bible speaks with authority because it is the word of God. It is the final rule for faith and practice because it is the inspired and trustworthy witness to the mighty acts of God in self-revelation and redemption, all brought to fulfillment in the life, teachings, and saving

work of Jesus Christ. It reveals the mind of Christ and teaches the meaning of his lordship. In its unique and unified disclosure of the will of God for humankind, the Bible is the final authority in pointing persons to Christ and in guiding them in all matters of Christian faith and moral duty. The responsibility must be accepted to study the Bible with an open and reverent mind, to seek the meaning of its message through research and prayer, and to bring one's life under the discipline of its instruction.

The Bible as the inspired revelation of God's will and way, made full and complete in the life and teachings of Christ, is our authoritative rule of faith and practice.

3. *The Holy Spirit*

The Holy Spirit is God actively present in the world and, particularly, in human experience. He is God revealing himself and his will to people. The Spirit therefore is the voice of divine authority. He is the Spirit of Christ, and his authority is the will of Christ. Inasmuch as the Scriptures came into being as humans inspired by the Spirit spoke for God, the truth of the Bible expresses the will of the Spirit and is apprehended by the illumination of the Spirit. He convicts people of sin and of righteousness and of judgment, thus making effective for individual salvation the saving work of Christ. He abides in the heart of the believer acting as the believer's advocate with God and God's interpreter to people. He calls the believer to trust and obedience and thereby produces in the believer's life the fruits of holiness and love.

The Spirit seeks to achieve God's will and purpose among people. He empowers Christians for the work of ministry and sanctifies and preserves the redeemed for the praise of Christ. He calls for a free and dynamic response to the lordship of Christ and for a creative and faithful obedience to the Word of God.

The Holy Spirit is God actively revealing himself and his will to people. He therefore interprets and confirms the voice of divine authority.

II. The Individual

1. The Individual's Worth

The Bible reveals that each human being is created in the image of God—is unique, precious, and irreplaceable. Created a rational being, each person is morally responsible to God and other human beings. A human as an individual is distinguishable from all other persons. As a person, the individual is bound with others in the bundle of life, for no one lives or dies to self.

The Bible also reveals that Christ died for all. The fact that humans were created in the image of God and that Christ died for them is the source of human worth and dignity. A human has the God-given right to be recognized and accepted as an individual regardless of race, color, creed, or culture; to belong with dignity and respect to his or her community; and to have the full opportunity to achieve individual potentiality.

Every individual is created in the image of God and therefore merits respect and consideration as a person of infinite dignity and worth.

2. The Individual's Competence

The individual, because created in the image of God, is responsible for moral and religious decisions. The individual is competent under the leadership of the Holy Spirit to make a personal response to God's call in the gospel of Christ, to commune with God, and to grow in the grace and knowledge of our Lord. With the individual's competence is linked the responsibility to seek the truth and, having found it, to act upon it and to share it with others. While there can properly be no coercion in religion, the Christian is never free to be neutral in matters of conscience and conviction.

Each person is competent under God to make his or her own moral and religious decisions and is responsible to God in all matters of moral and religious duty.

3. The Individual's Freedom

Baptists cherish freedom of conscience and full freedom of religion for all persons. The individual is free to accept or reject religion; to

choose or change faith; to preach and teach the truth as she or he sees
it, always with due regard for the rights and convictions of others; to
worship both privately and publicly; to invite others to share in services of worship and church activities; and to own property and all
needed facilities with which to propagate his or her faith. Such
religious liberty is cherished not as a privilege to be granted, denied,
or merely tolerated—either by the state or by any religious body—
but as a right under God.

*Every person is free under God in all matters of conscience and has
the right to embrace or reject religion and to witness to religious beliefs,
always with proper regard for the rights of other persons.*

II. The Christian Life

1. Salvation by Grace
Grace is God's loving and merciful provision for the need of lost
people. People in their natural state are self-centered and proud; they
are in bondage to Satan and spiritually dead in trespasses and sins.
Because of their sinful nature, people are helpless to save themselves.
But God is graciously disposed toward all in spite of their moral cor-
ruption and spiritual rebellion. Salvation is not the result of human
merit or achievement but of divine purpose and initiative. It is not
by means of sacramental meditation or moral training but by divine
mercy and power. Salvation from sin is the free gift of God through
Jesus Christ, conditioned only upon repentance toward God and trust
in and commitment to Christ the Lord.

Salvation, which comes by grace, through faith, brings one into a
vital life-changing union with Christ, which is characterized by a life
of holiness and good works. The same grace by means of which one
has been saved is the assurance of God's continuing forgiveness and
help in living the Christian life.

*Salvation from sin is the free gift of God through Jesus Christ, condi-
tioned only upon trust in and commitment to Christ the Lord.*

2. The Demands of Discipleship

Christian discipleship begins with a commitment to Christ as Lord. It develops as one abides in Christ and obeys his commands. The disciple learns the truth of Christ only by becoming obedient to it. This obedience demands the surrender of selfish ambitions and purposes and requires obedience to the will of the Father. Obedience led Christ to the cross and requires that each disciple take up his or her own cross and follow him.

Cross-bearing or self-denial will be expressed in many ways in the life of the disciple. The disciple will seek first the kingdom of God. The disciple's supreme loyalty will be to Christ. The disciple will be faithful to the commission of Christ. The disciple's personal life will manifest self-discipline, purity, integrity, and Christian love in every relationship. Christian discipleship is all-inclusive.

The demands of Christian discipleship, based on the recognition of the lordship of Christ, relate to the whole of life and call for full obedience and complete devotion.

3. The Priesthood of the Believer

Every person is competent to go directly to God for forgiveness through repentance and faith. That person needs neither individual nor church to dispense salvation. There is but one mediator of God and people, Jesus Christ our Lord. After one has become a Christian, one has direct access to God through Christ. The Christian has entered into a royal priesthood and is privileged to minister for Christ to all. Christians are to share with them the faith they cherish and to serve them in the name and spirit of their Lord. The priesthood of believers, therefore, means that all members serve as equals under God in the fellowship of a local church.

Each Christian, having direct access to God through Christ, is his or her own priest and is also under obligation to become a priest for Christ on behalf of other persons.

4. The Christian and the Home

The home is God's basic unit in society. The building of enduring Christian homes should be of primary concern to all believers in

Christ. Such homes are built upon the union of a Christian man and a Christian woman who are emotionally, spiritually, and physically mature, and who are bound by a deep and genuine love. The two should share similar ideals and ambitions and should be dedicated to the rearing of their children in the instruction and discipline of the Lord. This calls for regular Bible study and family worship in the home. In such homes, the spirit of Christ permeates all the relations of the family.

Churches are under obligation to guide and prepare young people for marriage, to train and aid parents in their responsibilities, to help parents and children face adequately the tests and crises of life, to assist those who suffer from broken homes, and to help the bereaved and aged to find continuing significance in life.

The home is basic in God's purpose for human well-being, and the development of Christian family life should be a supreme concern of all believers in Christ.

5. The Christian as a Citizen

The Christian is a citizen of two worlds—the kingdom of God and the political state—and should be obedient to the law of the land as well as the higher law of God. If a choice must be made, the Christian must obey God rather than humans. A Christian should be respectful to those who interpret and enforce the law; and a Christian should participate actively in the life of the community, seeking to permeate social, economic, and political life with Christian spirit and principles. The Christian's stewardship of life includes such citizenship responsibilities as paying taxes, voting, and supporting worthy legislation. The Christian should pray for those in authority and should encourage other Christians to accept civic responsibility as a service to God and others.

The Christian is a citizen of two worlds—the kingdom of God and the state—and should be obedient to the law of the land as well as to the higher law of God.

IV. The Church

1. Its Nature

In the New Testament the term church designates God's people in their totality or in local assembly. The church is a fellowship of persons redeemed in Christ Jesus, divinely called, divinely created, and made one under the sovereign rule of God. The church as a local body—an organism indwelt by the Holy Spirit—is a fellowship of baptized believers, voluntarily banded together for worship, study, mutual discipline, Christian service, and the propagation of the gospel at home and abroad.

The church, in its inclusive sense, is the fellowship of persons redeemed by Christ and made one in the family of God. The church, in its local sense, is a fellowship of baptized believers, voluntarily banded together for worship, nurture, and service.

2. Its Membership

The church in local embodiment is a fellowship of regenerated and baptized believers associated by covenant in the faith and fellowship of the gospel. Properly, one qualifies for church membership by being begotten of God and by voluntarily accepting baptism. For such persons membership in a local church becomes a holy privilege and a sacred study. Simply to be enrolled in the membership of a church does not constitute membership in the body of Christ. The utmost care should be exercised to see that persons are accepted into the fellowship of a church only on reasonable evidence of regeneration and true commitment to Christ as Lord.

Membership in a church is a privilege properly extended only to regenerated persons who voluntarily accept baptism and commit them-selves to faithful discipleship in the body of Christ.

3. Its Ordinances

Baptism and the Lord's Supper are the two ordinances of the church. They are symbolic, but their observance involves faith, confession, self-examination, discernment, gratitude, dedication, fellowship, and worship.

Baptism is to be administered by the church under the authority of the triune God and is the immersion in water of those who by faith have received Jesus as Saviour and Lord. In that act the believer is portrayed as buried with Christ and raised with him to walk in newness of life.

The Lord's Supper, observed through the symbols of the bread and the cup, is a sober searching of one's heart, a thankful remembrance of Christ and his sacrificial death on the cross, a blessed assurance of his return, and a joyous fellowship with the living Christ and his people.

Baptism and the Lord's Supper, the two ordinances of the church, are symbolic of redemption, but their observance involves spiritual realities in personal Christian experience.

4. Its Government

The controlling principle of government for a local church is the lordship of Christ. The autonomy of the church rests upon the fact that Christ is present in and is the head of each congregation of his people. The church cannot, therefore, be subordinate to the rule of any other religious body. Autonomy, thus, is valid only when exercised under the lordship of Christ.

Democracy, or congregational government, is proper to the extent that, led by the Holy Spirit, it provides and calls for free and responsible participation in the deliberations and work of the church. Neither a majority nor a minority, nor even unanimity, necessarily reflects God's will.

A church is an autonomous body, subject only to Christ, its head. Its democratic government, properly, reflects the equality and responsibility of believers under the lordship of Christ.

5. Its Relation to the State

Both church and state are ordained of God and are answerable to him. Each is distinct: each has a divine purpose; neither is to encroach upon the rights of the other. They are to remain separate, but they are to stand in proper relationship with each other under God. The state is ordained of God for the exercise of civil authority, the maintenance of order, and the promotion of public welfare.

The church is a voluntary fellowship of Christians, joined together under the lordship of Christ for worship and service in his name. The state is not to ignore God's sovereignty or reject his laws as the basis for moral order and social justice. Christians are to accept their responsibilities for the support of the state and for loyal obedience to civil authority in all things not contrary to the clear will of God.

The state owes the church protection and full freedom in the pursuit of its spiritual ends. The church owes the state moral and spiritual reinforcement for law and order and the clear proclamation of those truths which undergird justice and peace. The church is responsible both to pray for the state and to declare the judgments of God as they relate to government, responsible citizenship, and the rights of all persons. The church must take seriously and practice consistently the principles which it declares should govern the relation of church and state.

Church and state are both ordained of God and are answerable to him. They should remain separate, but they are under the obligation of mutual recognition and reinforcement as each seeks to fulfil its divine function.

6. *Its Relation to the World*

Jesus Christ came into the world, but he was not of the world. He prayed not that his people be taken out of the world but that they be kept from evil. His church, therefore, is to be responsibly in the world but not of the world. The church and individual Christians must oppose evil and work toward the elimination of all that corrupts or degrades the life of people. It must take a positive stand for righteousness and work earnestly to bring about mutual respect, sisterhood and brotherhood, justice, and peace in all the relationships of people and races and nations. It looks forward with confidence to the ultimate fulfillment of God's purpose in Christ for the world.

The church is to be responsibly in the world; its mission is to the world; but its character and ministry are not to be of the world.

V. Our Continuing Task

These ideals, which have brought to focus the distinctive witness of
Baptists, impinge on the current situation with crucial significance.
Forces in the world challenge them. Trends in our churches and in
our denomination endanger them. If these ideals are to inspire
Baptists with a sense of mission worthy of the present hour, they must
be related with dynamic reality to every aspect of our continuing task.

1. Centrality of the Individual

Baptists historically have placed emphasis on the worth of the individual, giving the individual a central place in the work of their
churches and denomination. This distinctive, however, is endangered
in this day of automation and pressures to conformity. Alert to these
dangers within their own ranks as well as in the world, Baptists should
make sure that the individual's integrity is preserved.

The individual's high value should be reflected in our worship
services, evangelistic work, missionary labors, stewardship emphasis,
teaching and training program, and Christian education. Programs
are justified by what they do for persons reached by them. This means,
among other things, that the individual should never be used as a
mere means, never manipulated, and never treated simply as a statistic.
This requires, rather, that we give primary consideration to the individual's supreme worth, moral freedom, urgent needs, and potential
for Christ.

*The individual's worth, the individual's needs and moral freedom,
and the individual's potential for Christ should have primary consideration in the life and work of our churches.*

2. Worship

The worship of God, whether personal or corporate, is the highest
expression of Christian faith and devotion. It is supreme both in privilege and in duty. Baptists face an urgent need to improve the quality
of their worship so that they may experience corporately a renewal of
faith, hope, and love from communion with a great and loving God.

Worship must be in keeping with the nature of God as the Holy One. Therefore, it must be an experience of adoration and confession expressed with reverential awe and humility. Worship is not mere form and ritual but an experience of the living God through holy meditation and self-giving. It is not merely a religious service but communion with God in the reality of praise, in the sincerity of love, and in the beauty of holiness.

Worship becomes most meaningful when in reverence and orderliness it combines the inspiration of the presence of God, the proclamation of the gospel, and the freedom of the Spirit. The result of such worship will be a stronger awareness of the holiness and majesty and grace of God, greater devotion to him, and fuller commitment to his will.

Worship—which involves an experience of communion with the living and holy God—calls for a new emphasis on reverence and orderliness, on confession and humility, and on awareness of the holiness and majesty and grace and purpose of God.

3. The Christian Ministry

The church and all of its members are in the world to serve. In one sense, every child of God is called to minister as a Christian. However, there has been widespread failure to emphasize adequately the uniqueness of the call to vocational Christian service. An emphasis at this point is particularly pertinent in view of the pressure on highly competent young people to enter scientific and related fields and also because of the decreasing number of young people who are responding to God's call to vocational Christian work.

Those who have been called by the Lord into the Christian ministry should realize that their basic call is a mandate to serve. They are in a special sense slaves of Christ and are his ministers in the churches and to the people. They should magnify their responsibilities rather than their special privileges. Their distinctive functions are not for the purpose of vainglory but are means whereby they serve God, the church, and their fellow men.

Churches are responsible under God for those whom they ordain. They should maintain high standards for those seeking ordination as to Christian experience, Christian character, and the conviction of a divine call. They should also encourage those ordained to seek adequate training for their work.

Every Christian is under obligation to minister or to serve with complete self-giving, but God in his wisdom calls many persons in a unique way to dedicate their lives to a full-time church-related ministry.

4. Evangelism

Evangelism is the proclamation of God's judgment on sin and of the good news of God's grace in Jesus Christ. Evangelism is the response of Christians to persons in the bondage of evil and to the charge of Christ that his followers are to be his witnesses to all people. It declares that the gospel and the gospel alone is the power of God for salvation. The task of evangelism is primary in the mission of the church and in the vocation of every Christian.

Evangelism thus conceived calls for a firm theological foundation and for unfailing emphasis on the basic doctrines of salvation. New Testament evangelism is evangelism by means of the gospel and by the power of the Spirit. It aims at the saving of the whole person. It confronts the lost with the cost of discipleship and the claims of the lordship of Christ. It magnifies divine grace, voluntariness of faith, and reality in the experience of conversion.

Invitations to unsaved persons should never minimize these imperative realities. The manipulation of individuals, use of the tricks of mass psychology, cheap substitutes for conviction, and all vainglorious schemes are a sin against God and a sin against lost persons. The constraining love of Christ, the doom of the unsaved, and the strength of sin constitute a compelling urgency.

Personal and mass evangelism, church centered evangelism, the use of sound methods and every worthy medium, the witness of personal piety and a Christlike spirit, agonizing intercession for the mercy and power of God, and utter dependence on the Holy Spirit point the way to the kind of evangelism desperately needed for this critical time.

Evangelism which is primary in the mission of the church and the vocation of every Christian, is the proclamation of God's judgment and grace in Jesus Christ and the call to accept and follow him as Lord.

5. Missions

Missions, as we use the term, is the extension of God's redemptive purpose through evangelism, education, and Christian service beyond the local church. The lost masses of the world constitute a stirring challenge to Christian churches.

Since Baptists believe in the freedom and competence of each person to make individual decisions in matters of religion, it is our responsibility under God to see that each individual has the knowledge and opportunity to make the right decision. We are under the compulsion of the divine commission to proclaim the gospel to every person of every race and nation. The urgency of the present world situation, the aggressive appeal of competing faiths and ideologies, and our concern for the lost call us to dedicate our utmost in people and money to proclaim the redemption of Christ to the world.

Co-operation in world missions is imperative. We must use every means at our disposal, including the modern media of mass communication, to give Christ to the world. We cannot rely exclusively on a small, specially trained and dedicated group of missionaries. Every Baptist is a missionary, no matter where he or she lives or what his or her position or vocation may be. Our personal and group acts and attitudes towards those of other nations, races, and religions are part of our testimony for or against Christ. Our witness in every realm and relationship of life must lend credence to our proclamation that Jesus Christ is Lord of all.

Missions seeks the extension of God's redemptive purpose in all the world through evangelism, education, and Christian service and calls for the utmost dedication on the part of Christians to this task.

6. Stewardship

Christian stewardship is the responsible employment under God of one's life, talents, time, and material substance in the proclamation of the gospel and in Christian service. In the sharing of the gospel, stewardship finds its highest meaning. Stewardship is based on the acknowledgment that all we are and have comes from God as a sacred trust.

Material possessions in themselves are neither good nor evil. The love of money rather than money itself is the root of all kinds of evil. In Christian stewardship, money becomes the means to spiritual ends both for the one who gives and for those who receive. Accepted as a sacred trust, money becomes not a threat but an opportunity. Jesus was concerned that people be free from the tyranny of material things and that they use material things to serve their own needs and the needs of others.

The responsibility of stewardship applies not only to the individual Christian but also to each local church, convention, agency, and institution of the denomination. What is intrusted to each individual or institution is not to be hoarded nor spent selfishly but administered wisely in the service of humankind and to the glory of God.

Christian stewardship conceives the whole of life as a sacred trust from God and requires the responsible use of life, time, talents, and substance— personal and corporate—in the service of Christ.

7. *Teaching and Training*

Teaching and training are central in Christ's commission to his followers. The nature of the Christian faith and the nature of Christian experience constitute a divine imperative to teach and train. Teaching and training are necessary to the development of Christian attitudes, the demonstration of Christian virtues, the enjoyment of Christian privileges, the fulfillment of Christian responsibilities, and the achievement of Christian certainty. Teaching and training should begin at birth and continue throughout life. They are divinely ordained functions of the home and the church. They are the way toward Christian maturity.

Since faith must be personal and every response to the lordship of Christ must be voluntary, teaching and training are prerequisites to responsible Christian discipleship and to a vital Christian witness. This means that the educational task of the church is central. The test of the teaching and training ministry is the extent to which it results in Christlikeness and in the ability to deal effectively with the moral, social, and spiritual issues of the contemporary world. We must teach and train that persons may know the truth that makes them free, experience the love that makes them servants of humankind, and achieve the faith that imparts hope in the kingdom of God.

The nature of Christian faith and Christian experience and the nature and needs of persons make teaching and training imperative.

8. Christian Education

Faith and reason stand together in true knowledge. Genuine faith seeks intelligent understanding and expression. Christian schools should keep faith and reason in proper balance. This means that they should not be satisfied with anything less than the highest academic standards. At the same time, they should provide a distinctive type of education—an education thoroughly infused with the Christian spirit, permeated by the Christian perspective, and dedicated to genuine Christian values.

Our Christian schools have a responsibility to train and inspire men and women for effective lay and vocational leadership in our churches and in the world. The churches, in turn, have a responsibility to support adequately all their educational institutions.

The members of our churches should be interested in those who teach in their own institutions and in what they teach. It should be recognized that there are limits to academic freedom; it should also be recognized that teachers in our institutions should have adequate freedom for creative scholarship. This freedom can be and should be balanced by a deep sense of personal responsibility to God, to the truth, to the denomination, and to the constituency they serve.

Christian education grows out of the relation of faith and reason and calls for academic excellence and freedom that are both real and responsible.

9. Self-Criticism

Both the local church and the denomination, if they are to remain healthy and fruitful, must accept the responsibility of constructive self-criticism. It would be damaging to our churches and to our denomination to deny the right to differ or to consider that our methods and policies are final and perfect. The work of our churches and of our denomination needs frequent re-evaluation to prevent the sterility of traditionalism. This is particularly true in the area of methods, but it also applies to historic principles and practices as they relate to contemporary life. This means that our churches and denominational institutions and agencies should defend and protect the right of our people to question and to criticize constructively.

Healthy self-criticism will center on basic issues and will thus save us from the disintegrating effects of accusation and recrimination. For one to criticize does not necessarily mean that one is disloyal; criticism may stem from a deep commitment to the welfare of the denomination. Such criticism will aim at growth toward full maturity both for the individual and the denomination.

Every Christian group, if it is to remain healthy and fruitful, must accept the responsibility of constructive self-criticism.

"THE PEOPLE CALLED AMERICAN BAPTISTS: A CONFESSIONAL STATEMENT"

[Certainly one of the most beautifully and artistically written statements on the Baptist identity is this one from the American Baptist Churches, U.S.A. The result of the "Commission on Denominational Identity," this confessional statement is only one part of the Commission's report entitled "American Baptists: A Unifying Vision." Christocentric in character, the statement weaves historic Baptist principles together with biblical and theological affirmations to describe contemporary American Baptists. Ralph H. Elliott served as Chair of the Commission that drafted the document. This document and other parts of the Commission's report are published in the American Baptist Quarterly, *volume VI, number 2, June, 1987.]*

"THE PEOPLE CALLED AMERICAN BAPTISTS: A CONFESSIONAL STATEMENT"

American Baptists affirm that God is sovereign over all and that this sovereignty is expressed and realized through Jesus Christ. Therefore, we affirm the Lordship of Christ over the world and the Church. We gladly confess that Jesus Christ is Savior and Lord. We are called in loyalty to Jesus Christ to proclaim the Good News of God's sovereign, reconciling grace, and to declare the saving power of the Gospel to every human being and to every human institution. We celebrate Christ's charge to "make disciples of all nations" and to bear witness to God's redeeming Reign in human affairs.

American Baptists are summoned to this mission in common with all Christians everywhere. With the whole Body of Christ, we also believe that God has been revealed in Jesus Christ as in no other, and that "God was in Christ reconciling the world to Himself"

(2 Cor 5:18). We anticipate the day when every creature and all creation, on earth and beyond, will confess that Jesus Christ is Lord.

American Baptists further believe that God has given this particular community of believers called Baptists a distinctive history and experience. As we share much in common with all Christians everywhere, so Baptists everywhere celebrate a common heritage. Within that larger Baptist family, American Baptists possess certain "convictional genes" which direct our special task and ministry.

Therefore
With Baptist brothers and sisters across the world:
   We believe
      —That the Bible is a trustworthy and final authority for faith and practice when interpreted responsibly under the guidance of God's Holy Spirit within the community of faith,
      —That the Church is a gathered fellowship of regenerated believers, a sign of the coming universal Reign of God,
      —That the Freedom to respond to the Lordship of Christ in all circumstances is fundamental to the Christian Gospel and to human dignity, and
      —That Evangelism is the ongoing task of every Christian and of every Church.

Accordingly, as American Baptists
   We affirm
      —That God through Jesus Christ calls us to be
         • A Contemporary People
            —who have a remembrance for the past and a vision for the future,
            —who, committed to religious liberty and to the separation of church and state, challenge our present world in all of its political, social and moral values.

- A Biblical People
    - —who affirm the centrality of Scripture through independent reading as confirmed and understood within the community of believers,
    - —who pursue the study of God's inspired Word as a mandate for living.
- An Inclusive People
    - —who, gifted by a plurality of backgrounds, find unity in diversity and diversity in unity,
    - —who embrace a pluralism of race, ethnicity, gender and theology,
    - —who represent individual differences of conviction, and
    - —who bring the free church tradition to cooperative and ecumenical Christianity.
- A Redeemed People
    - —who herald forth the vision of a redeemed world,
    - —who gather as a believer's Church,
    - —who follow the Lord in believer's baptism,
    - —who share in the meal of the Kingdom known as the Lord's Supper,
    - —who live their faith as visible saints, and
    - —who honor the priesthood of all believers.
- An Interdependent People
    - —who live and work together "in association,"
    - —who gladly embody in our practice the ministry of the whole people of God, and
    - —who honor pastoral ministries.
- A Missional People
    - —who strive to fulfill the Great Commission,
    - —who engage in educational, social, and health ministries,
    - —who accept local and global responsibilities, and
    - —who affirm both individual redemption and corporate justice.

• A Worshiping People
  —who regularly gather to praise God,
  —who receive nourishment by communion with
     the Risen Christ,
  —who share an open and public confession of faith,
     and
  —who believe that private worship brings vitality to
     corporate celebration.

We Further Believe
  —That God has called us forth to such an hour as this,
  —That we live with a realizable hope,
  —That all things cohere in Christ,
  —That all creation will find its ultimate fulfillment in God,
  —That we shall see the One whose we are, and
  —That Jesus shall reign for ever and ever.

Made in the USA
Lexington, KY
15 March 2019